MANCHESTER UNITED

Also by Eric Thornton

MANCHESTER CITY
Meredith to Mercer

LEEDS UNITED
and Don Revie

MANCHESTER UNITED

Barson to Busby

ERIC THORNTON

ROBERT HALE · LONDON

First published in Great Britain 1971

ISBN 0 7091 2499 6

Robert Hale & Company
63 Old Brompton Road
London S.W.7.

PRINTED IN GREAT BRITAIN BY
BRISTOL TYPESETTING CO. LTD.
BARTON MANOR - ST. PHILIPS
BRISTOL

Contents

Illustrations

With the exception of the action shots of George Best, Bobby Charlton and the picture of Frank O'Farrell, supplied by Syndication International, all photographs were provided by *Manchester Evening News*.

ONE

Threepenny Cigars

ONE OF those dark, starless nights had settled peacefully over Old Trafford as Matt Busby said a cheery farewell, and Harold Hardman poured out a final drop of the hard stuff to strengthen me against a cold westerly breeze.

We were the last of the Mohicans in the boardroom after a midweek game. The Manchester United chairman, who had been quietly reviewing the past, guided me back into the stand and we looked quietly out over the silent, empty acres of seats and terracing picked out sharply by floodlights blazing down from encircling towers.

Hardman, who lived through the heartbreak up-and-down years between the wars said : " We've had to fight to reach this stage of affluence, but everybody associated with us will always go on fighting, which is why I'm so absolutely certain that no one or anything will ever destroy this club or ruin its image."

I was reminded of the remark, which he made just before his death a short while ago, when that unfortunate series of defeats around the turn of this year had some folk viewing the future most pessimistically. It's admitted it was a tough winter. It's admitted that those League and Cup defeats by Manchester City, Aston Villa, and Middlesbrough were shockers. Yet United's name still spells out football just as clearly in the capitals of the old and new worlds as it does in the plantations of China and India, the swamps of Burma, the rolling prairies of the Dominions, and the sands of the western desert.

Of course, it really did seem as if they had taken the full count in 1958, when most of the wonder team of that era was wiped out in the snows of a winter night while flying home from an Iron Curtain rendezvous. And nobody gave Busby much chance of surviving. But even then Hardman said to me as we returned from paying tribute to the dead on Granada TV : "This is not going to be the end, although it may seem so, because I'm determined the club will go on."

It did. Because Jimmy Murphy joined that grand fighter at the helm until the skipper eventually came home from the hospital in Munich, and the three together fought their way through new storms and tribulations to many brilliant triumphs in battles which were often staged thousands of miles apart.

In a way, that was no new experience. For this club has been down and almost out on other occasions. Indeed, twice the finger of the Registrar in Bankruptcy has almost beckoned them. Yet they have dodged the threat of closure each time because they always had life savers. And they have continued building a history which is so liberally dotted with personalities and accomplishments that when I was asked to trace its story from the very beginning even preliminary search of my own records indicated the size of the problem, and the difficulty of condensing everything into sixty thousand words.

It's a bittersweet trail which draws a switchback graph over the first sixty years or so, and then pinpoints fantastic successes at home and abroad until the very ground itself has become glamorised. It is as well known in Madrid, Berlin, Lisbon, Moscow, Montreal, New York and all the other international centres as it is in the back streets of Salford, Stretford, Bolton, Stockport and Collyhurst.

Let's go. Yes, and right back to the days of threepenny cigars, eighteen bob Savile Row overcoats, penny match programmes, and that period in time when Bootle, Burton United and Darwen were contesting the honours of the Football League.

It was the eighties of the last century, and the railwaymen in the shunting yards to the north of Manchester, who were employed by the old Lancashire and Yorkshire Railway

Company, were forming their very own L & Y Football Club. And, believe it or not, they actually began writing its history with a High Court action which ended in their favour. They were awarded damages for slander against a Birmingham player, yet immediately regretted tangling with the law because their costs were high, and the damages amounted to only *one farthing*.

You may guess that set the scene for tough talking in committee. Some suggested throwing up the sponge. But rescuers arrived, changed the name, and they were off once again—off as Newton Heath L Y R Cricket and Football Club.

It was 1888, a time when Sir Matthew Busby wasn't even a sparkle in his father's eye. Come to that, another important contributor to the club's later record was just a babe in arms—George Bedford, that delightful character who was always resurrecting old newspaper cuttings about vital years whenever we met for the odd elbow raiser in his Prestwich hostelry.

There were others, of course. To wit John Henry Davies. Woe to anybody attempting obstruction of his plans once he had fallen in love with the club and the game. It is a name that won't mean very much to most presentday supporters. I'll gamble that hardly more than a handful of the Stretford Enders have heard of J.H.D., as he was then known around the family brewery of Walker and Humphries. Yet it is fair to say that the Old Trafford ground is almost a memorial to his tremendous endeavours for the club in its teething years.

I would actually go so far as to suggest that Manchester United would have folded in the early part of this century but for J.H.D., and, in a smaller way, the brewery company's young accountant. He was a fellow by the name of George Lawton, who always used to lock up the office and cycle over to Newton Heath on Saturday afternoons. That routine was never changed whether it was snowing, raining, or blowing half a gale.

George was absorbed in the poor little struggling club, with its pitiful ramshackle headquarters, a mud heap of a pitch which was often enshrouded in smoke, and changing rooms at " The Three Crowns ", in Oldham Road, nearly a quarter of a mile away. He was one of their keenest backers as they landed a place in the Football League, in 1892, when two divisions were formed, and " Test " matches at the end of each season decided which of the bottom clubs should be relegated.

Some of the malcontents wanted to change the club's name again, but the idea had a mixed reception. Loyalists set their faces against the plan, content to see their beloved Newton Heath operating in the League, even though many of the other clubs were hitting them for six, and relegation was their lot in 1894.

It was a struggle climbing out of the Second Division, and they stayed inferior to such teams as Bury, Notts County, Grimsby Town, Lincoln City, Glossop North End, Burton United and Chesterfield until, in 1902, they became Manchester United, and somehow fought harder and better, without paying their way. Lack of cover on wintry days was one big reason for thin crowds, and George and Harry Stafford, the skipper, worried over it. One day, George was cycling to a Saturday game when a fellow in a horse and trap knocked him off his old iron. He ended up on all fours, biting the dust of Oldham Road. Yet he couldn't say a strong piece to the culprit because, on looking up, he discovered it was his boss, driving home for a late lunch.

The Great One leaned over, inquired where his clerk was going in such a hurry, and was apparently astonished to learn of his enthusiasm for football, and for one particular club. Getting away as quickly as possible, George arrived at the ground to be staggered with the news that the bailiffs had moved in, stationed themselves alongside each of the three turnstiles, and were taking the cash as soon as it was handed over by the fans.

It was a tricky position. Definitely, it seemed as if the curtains were on their way down at last. George and the skipper talked it over after the game, bravely decided to cycle to J.H.D's home, and took their courage in both hands. They put over such a case that the brewery chief went to look over the old place after confessing that he had never seen a game of football.

He paid off all the debts and became a fanatical supporter. To such degree that he spent freely on ground improvements, and added a small covered section for the private use of his own family and immediate friends. Cash worries vanished into thin air. More went to watch, and better players joined up as they heard of generous benefits.

It all meant that everybody got paid. Gone were those days when one of them had to stay at home all Sunday because his best suit was in pawn in the absence of any wages. More and more crowded round for places on the gravy train, though a note of caution was sounded by the F.A. after hearing that *The Great One* had crossed the team's palms with golden sovereigns in celebration of one particularly fine victory.

It didn't really matter in those far-off days. The style had been set, and after regaining their lost First Division spot in 1906, the team developed all-round strength, and walked off with the club's first championship in 1908. Actually, they won that title nearly two months before the end of the season, and finally finished eleven points ahead of their nearest challengers, Aston Villa—and, hold your breath, *Manchester City*!

Thousands rallied as they set off on the next campaign. The title eluded them that time round, but nobody worried because the boys fought their way to a Cup Final with Bristol City, at Crystal Palace, and a solitary goal from Sandy Turnbull won them the coveted trophy.

The oldtimers will remember that the inseparable Duckworth, Roberts and Bell formed the half-back line with tremendous distinction for many years. But I wonder how may could unhesitatingly identify the right-winger? It was the great Billy Meredith. The boy from the Denbighshire village of Chirk, whom Manchester City first groomed into an international star, and had to release when the F.A. imposed suspensions after an inquiry into charges alleging illegal payments. He and Turnbull and Herbert Burgess and Jimmy Bannister all joined United.

Meredith was one of the greatest wingers the game has ever known. A scoring winger, too. He not only played in 686 League and Cup games for City and United, but also hit 287 goals. How many other wingers have done that? Or come even near such a performance? If you check, I'll gamble you won't need more than the fingers of one hand.

He lived in the days when players were very happy to pocket a quid. Often, he cycled to and from his Welsh home to Manchester on match days, and thought nothing of it. A winger in the old fashioned style he began collecting international caps way back in 1895, and was still in his country's line-up against England, Scotland and Ireland in 1920. Like Ceasar's Gaul, his early life was divided into three parts—Wales, City and United.

Meredith's trademark was the toothpick, which he was always using, but though generally a willing talker he somehow dried up when I took him along as an extra commentator for the Wembly final between Burnley and Charlton, in 1947. The idea was that I should phone through a continuous report, merely halting every ten minutes or so for his additional opinion. We began nicely. When I turned to him he said : " Burnley are covering well against the long 'uns, but Charlton are using the ball better ". Very good. I spun that out into three paragraphs, and resumed my own move-by-move account.

Ten minutes later I questioned him again, but he said almost the same thing. So I pressed for new points the next time, and thought I'd got through, especially when he selected a new pick from his little pack. But I hadn't. For on the half hour he came back to me just the same as before : " Burnley are covering well . . ." I let him go on enjoying himself, and added occasional paragraphs on his behalf. He obviously didn't feel in the mood for the unaccustomed rôle of sportswriter instead of player.

Yet on the way home in the night train he talked well, and laughingly recounted the time when a bootlace broke, and he went to the trainer's bench for another. Noticing one of the opposing players sitting down alongside, Meredith asked if he was hurt, and the player said : " I'm not hurt, but I was told to mark you very closely, and that's what I am bloody well going to do."

Winning the Cup for the first time made J.H.D. as proud as the proverbial peacock, and the success of those two years set this wealthy businessman thinking so deeply about the future that he finally decided the club needed a better image. He picked the Old Trafford site, approved the plans, and met a bill of around £60,000 which was big money in those times.

It was decided that the official opening should be an occasion to be remembered and cherished by everybody, and was fixed for 19th February 1910. Liverpool were scheduled to be first visitors as old friends and rivals. On that particular day, however, they were not so friendly. For, after sharing a welcoming roll of drums and cheers from a crowd of over 50,000, the Merseysiders had the confounded temerity to beat United by 3-2.

Life became very good around that part of the world, and when the boys carried off the championship again in 1911, *The Great One* was in the seventh heaven of delight. To such degree that he handed out gold medals which had been specially struck, booked a coach and four for a day's racing at Chester, then brought them all back for a slap-up dinner at his home in Cheadle, with continuous music supplied on the lawn by the local brass band.

A crowd of talented players was by then assembled at Old Trafford, yet, strangely, the team began slipping after a wonderful run, and then almost dived out of the First Division just before war broke out in 1914. Spurs and Chelsea went over the edge, only a single point saving United, and, for a matter of extra interest, Bolton Wanderers, too.

Around that period some of the backroom boys did a bit of a shuffle. Jack Mangnall went back over his traces and rejoined City, while United handed their job of secretary-manager to a jovial bowler hatted character by the name of Jack Robson, whose lasting claim to fame was that he shaped into successes such as Lal Hilditch, Ray Bennion, Jack Silcock, Jackie Mew, Joe Spence, and, of course, signed the never-to-be-forgotten Frank Barson.

Barson! One of the really big names just after the first World War. In his Aston Villa days he played alongside Billy Walker, Andy Ducat, Clem Stephenson, and Sam Hardy. Taking over after Roberts had departed from the United team, he effectively blocked the mid-field gap.

When J.H.D. got him, he promised Barson a pub if he helped them back into the top circle from which they had just been relegated, and when they climbed up once more, Frank was given the managership of licensed premises in Ardwick. He took over one mid-day, and in next to no time at all the whole place was packed to the doors with fans all wanting to shake his hand, touch his shoulder, or buy him a drink. He struggled upstairs, quickly saw the obvious dangers, and handed the place over to the head barman—within one hour!

A strong-man centre-half, he had such a remarkable reputation for sturdy defence that most referees paid him particular attention. Once, when he stood down just before the start of a game at Bolton, and an unknown reserve took over and floored a Bolton forward the referee, none other than Stanley Rous, later knighted as F.A. Secretary, and now President of F.I.F.A., dashed up and said: "Cut that stuff out, Barson, or you're off next time."

Whenever Spence was moving up with the attack the fans always shouted "Give it to Joe". He was one of Robson's favourites. "Cocky" Hunter, whom Mangnall had signed from Chelsea the previous season, was very definitely not, and quickly transferred to Oldham Athletic, who were a power in the land some years back.

Well, as I was saying, this feller Hunter moved to Boundary Park, and unfortunately things didn't go too well for him. The Latics' secretary-manager of that time, well built moustachioed David Ashworth decided on changes because too many points were being dropped. He left Hunter out of the team.

That rocked the lad. He walked briskly over to his digs, armed himself with a pistol, returned to the ground, knocked on the manager's office door, and when Ashworth appeared he fired at his feet. Was that man scared? He banged the door closed, and everybody in Oldham who is a bit long in the tooth swears to this day that Ashworth wasn't seen for a week!

TWO

No Christmas Wages

George Bedford was a rabid supporter of the club years before he even wore long 'uns, and right up to the time of his death at the ripe old age of 84 in 1970, he considered there was only one professional soccer club in Britain, and that was Manchester United.

He could fairly claim to know the club from both sides of the fence, so to speak, because in his time as boy and man he had shinned over the wall for a free view, queued to pay his nimble tanner for admission, served as a scout who travelled thousands of miles and was often out of pocket on his expenses, and also had a spell on the board.

That mixed but faithful adherence to the cause always gave him pleasure to recall, though he used to click his teeth in annoyance every time he thought of two particular players he missed—Alex James and Hughie Gallacher. Whenever we talked of olden days and the golden eras of those two brilliant Scots he always said: "I should never have missed 'em."

James, the baggy pants hero first of the Preston fans and then of those of Arsenal, had been quietly called south for a trial with North End but George felt he could persuade him to travel on to Manchester. Yet as he reached Edinburgh and walked out the station for a taxi to the youngster's home wee Alex was booking his ticket for the trip south.

On another occasion, he betook himself up to Newcastle for a look at young Gallacher, who was then merely learning the business, and while helping himself to a drop of bitter George was rather staggered to hear that Hughie used to like a Friday night and a pint or two before the Saturday game.

So he struck him off the list, and wished he hadn't a year or two afterwards because the famous Scottish centre-forward hit three of the best into United's net at St. James' Park—after having had a night out with his pals.

Louis Rocca, the chief scout, took a dim view of those errors, as he was entitled to do because, after all, he was acknowledged to be one of the top scouts in Britain for over half a century, and, like the Mounties, liked to think he always got his man.

It was because of Rocca's diligence and persistence, and the friendly backing of George, that United landed 19-year-old Spence, the boyo I mentioned in the previous chapter. He had been playing in junior soccer on Tyneside, and was always considered one of the cheapest and best captures the club made up to that time.

Another fine piece of work when the game was getting back on its feet after the first of the two world conflicts enabled them to sign Jack Silcock, the fullback who rendered such splendid service. Both Rocca and Bedford had separately watched the youngster in junior games, and agreed he was a great prospect. So they called at his home, but Mrs. Silcock, busily employed rearing a large family on a small wage, turned a deaf ear to suggestions that the boy should forget about an ordinary job and play football for a living. She had apparently heard peculiar stories of footballers who hit hard times, and, anyway, were never paid very well. She kept saying she wouldn't let Jack become a pro while all the time she was nursing the youngest of the Silcocks.

Came the moment when the baby had had enough of this cross talk, and began crying. That was the cue for Rocca. He stood up, slipped a half-crown into its little money box over the fireplace, and it quietened. Whether it had been frightened by Rocca suddenly leaning over it nobody knows. But the fact is that it stopped whimpering, and just gazed at him.

A little later, obviously tired of examining the visitors, the baby cried again, and once more became silent when Rocca popped a second coin into the box. Peace reigned once more for a while, and then there was another outburst, and Rocca, slightly annoyed, dropped a third half dollar into the box. Maybe that satisfied the young offshoot because it went to sleep, and Mrs. Silcock, at last agreeing there must be some cash in the game if folk could throw their money around like that, said her son could sign.

In his closing years, Louis, a very pleasant and shrewd personality whom I always found exceptionally entertaining and interesting in conversation, went into the ice-cream business, and there are many who still stick to the story that United actually signed Hugh McLenahan, another of the old stars, for a freezer of ice-cream—a " donation " to a Stockport bazaar after it had been discovered that the County Club had no hold on the boy because they had signed him on a Sunday, which was against the rules.

Of course, those were the days when all players wore boots with bulbous toe caps which were never touched with a brush or dubbin, like the rest of the leather, and some preferred thick strips instead of studs under the soles, especially on bone hard pitches. When teams came out of their dressing-rooms and clobbered their way down the corridors before going out onto the field it often sounded as if a battalion of the Highland Infantry was making its exit.

We youngsters always wanted new boots and shirts and footballs for Christmas and birthdays. Nothing else. But the toes had to be like cast-iron or we turned 'em down. And sharply. For if they were not how could we score goals like Joe Smith, Billy Walker, Charlie Buchan, Billy Gillespie, and the rest of the heroes? You see, the days of the slippers had not arrived, as Freddie Tilson never tired of telling me. He was one of the Manchester City greats at that time. So was Eric Brook. But what are they doing in a book about Manchester United, you may wonder. Because but for one of those strange quirks of fate they would have landed up at Old Trafford instead of Maine Road.

It's a story that has been kept very quiet over the years, but I think it should be told. If only in fairness to Rocca. For he would have signed both but for the United board. He had been looking around for extra forward talent in the twenties, and heard about a couple of likely lads in south Yorkshire.

Hopping over to Barnsley, Louis saw young Tilson and Brook tying up an opposing defence in a Second Division game. The Oakwell outfit was hard up, needed the money, and told him that they might be prepared to do a deal for the pair at £5,000, which was fairly small when one remembered that Sunderland had just paid £6,550 to Burnley for Bob Kelly.

Rocca dashed home with the terrific news, and then felt as if someone had tossed a bucket of ice-cold water over him because the directors said they hadn't got that kind of money available, and were not interested. Tilson and Brook went to City, and became two of their best ever signings. Louis never forgot that disappointment and many years later was still bemoaning to me the fact that the United board had not tried raising the wind and beaten City to it.

On another occasion, he dashed back for an entirely different reason. It was this way. He was marking time on the old Weaver Bridge, twixt Chester and Manchester, waiting for a youngster he had just watched playing for Northwich Victoria, when a well built six-footer in size twelves, and with fists the size of your head suddenly appeared out of the evening mist.

He was a Vics supporter, recognised Louis, guessed his mission, and growled : " If you don't get that next train back to Manchester you'll end up floating down the river ". Mister Rocca made absolutely certain of being on that particular train!

Between the wars, United had a remarkable existence. They were relegated and promoted three times, and lived through a period know as *The Five Black Years*. Those stretched from 1930 to 1935, at a time when Manchester City were hitting the high spots with successive Cup finals, and a chase after the championship.

United joined Leeds on the toboggan into the Second Division in April 1931, after having been up-and-down since the end of the Kaiser's War. That particular drop cost them thousands of supporters. No wonder, either, when you glance back at the results sheet for season 1930-31, because it confirms that they actually lost all their first twelve League games! Yes, sir. Down they went like ninepins, in rapid succession, and were fairly easy opposition for most teams.

No fewer than forty-six goals were hammered into their net within a mere eight weeks. These were the teams who triumphed either on their own pitches or at Old Trafford—Villa 4-3, Middlesbrough 3-1, Chelsea 6-2, Huddersfield 6-0, Newcastle 4-1, Sheffield Wednesday 3-0, Huddersfield 3-0, Grimsby Town 2-0, Manchester City 4-1, West Ham 5-1, Arsenal 2-1, Portsmouth 4-1. Padlocked to the bottom rung of the First Division long before the turn of the year, their unhappy fate was sealed eight weeks short of the end of the season. There was mourning crêpe everywhere, and very little sympathy, I'm afraid.

It was a winter of discontent which spread over the following summer and cut the attendances right from the start of the next campaign. Expenses mounted because even in those days Mister Rising Price was striding around, and receipts were diving. So much so that there was yet another crisis at Christmas, and instead of the usual jollifications the club almost had to put up the shutters for a second time.

The real blow fell five days before Christmas Eve, and it was one right between the eyes for Secretary Walter Crickmer. He wrote out a cheque for the weekly wages, and walked smartly to the bank as he always did. The boys chatted away in the twin dressing-rooms, happily awaiting their individual packets even though they were not doing their stuff out on the park. Within half-an-hour dear old Walter, a man who never liked disappointing anybody, returned, and explained that there was no money to distribute because the bank wouldn't hand out any more. So the players trudged wearily home, without even the turkeys which were usually handed around at that period. When all was balanced, the club was involved to the extent of about £30,000, which was big money at a time when few folk accepted fivers unless you wrote your name and address on the back, because a £5 note represented a man's wage in a good job.

It seemed as if the club was finally going to close, and the possibility shook everybody. Not only in Lancashire but in every part of the country. The life saver that time was James Gibson, a member of the clothing firm of Biggs, Jones, Gibson

Ltd., whose son Alan is the present vice-chairman. He called a special meeting to discuss and examine the position, and appealed for subscribers—a thousand to subscribe £10 each, and another thousand £5 each. But only eight people supported the idea.

Naturally, Gibson was very disappointed at such poor public response, yet he paid the Christmas wages, bought the birds, and became guarantor at the bank. He was bravely backing the club for the future, though I'm not certain that he would have done it if he'd known how things would turn out in the immediate years ahead. For the crowds stayed poor over succeeding seasons, and in 1934 United again almost went overboard. In this instance they just missed sliding into the Third Division. Yes, the *Third* Division.

Supporters were still trying to forget that dismal Autumn of 1930, when rough seas swept them onto the rocks once more. Frantic changes were made week after week by Scott Duncan, the worried manager, yet nothing halted the slide to the wrong end of the Second Division, and they became a team without hope. Folk gradually began accepting the unpleasant fact that Third Division soccer would soon be staged at Old Trafford. Then a glimmer of hope lit up the depressing scene. Because Millwall, another club in distress, was throwing away points with the generosity of a millionaire. So much so that when the last week of the season arrived the position at the foot of the Second Division read this way :

					GLS	
	P	W	D	L	F A	PTS
Millwall	41	11	11	19	39-66	33
Manchester United	41	13	6	22	57-85	32
Lincoln City	42	9	8	25	44-75	26

You'll note that United had just one more match to play. A mere ninety minutes in which to settle their fate. And that final fixture meant a 400-mile round trip to London, for a clash with—*Millwall.* Nothing could have been planned more dramatically, and, of course, it had all Britain talking.

Scott Duncan took the boys away for a few days. They

tuned up at delightful Bexhill-on-Sea. One day he ordered a cliff-top walk of four miles into neighbouring Hastings, and while everybody was resting in the sunshine the boss slipped away, and spent a couple of bob on a local palmist. The old woman looked at his hands, gazed into the crystal, and then said : " You want to stop worrying yourself because everything will turn out right for you very soon." It was a good forecast. Everything did turn out right. United beat Millwall by 2-0, and the East Londoners went down with Lincoln.

When the result was announced from the front door of the *Manchester Evening News* office thousands cheered in the streets, and then joined others outside the station, and waited to give the team a warm welcome home. There were so many thronging the platform entrance and approaches that a stranger could have been forgiven thinking United had just won the Cup, or something like that. Maybe it was relief, because none had fancied attending games with such lowly opposition as Accrington Stanley, Barrow, New Brighton, Crewe, Hartlepools, Walsall, and so on. For the record the line-up that historic day of The Great Escape was this : Hacking; Griffiths, Jones; Robertson, Vose, McKay; Cage, McLenahan, Ball, Hine, Manley.

It had also been a notable period for another reason : they adopted new colours. In a desperate bid to strike gold they obtained the League's approval to exchange their bright red shirts for maroon and white hoops in which they first played against Bury, at Old Trafford, on 3rd March 1934, and scored their initial home success in four months. Yet they reverted to their old colours for the start of the next season.

Those twin decades of the 'twenties and 'thirties certainly provided memorable chapters in the club's history. Another interesting one spotlighted Albert Pape, a centre-forward who returned home one Saturday night a changed man. He had left London on the morning train for Manchester intent on playing for Clapton Orient against United. Instead, he suddenly switched loyalties, and played *against* Orient!

It was a transfer which staggered everybody. Not a hint had leaked out. No one outside the board-room even knew that the club was looking for a new centre. And none of the

London club's officials mentioned the matter to Albert until they booked into the Queen's Hotel for lunch, and were greeted by three directors from Old Trafford. At that time, United were fiercely contesting the leadership of the Second Division with Leicester City, Derby County, Portsmouth and Chelsea. They had decided they needed more finishing power, and discovered that Orient, just a run-of-the-mill club, needed the cash for survival, and were willing and eager to talk business.

So the mid-day conference was arranged, terms were settled, and after Albert had said a staggered good-bye to his old clubmates, United's trio drove him to the ground to meet his new ones, and then handed him a red shirt, and told him to get busy scoring.

Of course, that kind of thing couldn't happen today, because there are new League rulings on time lags. But, nevertheless, you can no doubt imagine the mighty gasp of surprise from the crowded stands and terraces when the teams were announced, and Pape was dramatically switched from No. 9 in Orient's line-up to No. 9 in that of United.

THREE

Seven Ages of Matt

We were talking in the foyer of Manchester's Midland Hotel after a meeting of the County F.A's Disciplinary Committee, and James Gibson suddenly said to me: "Keep this under your hat, but I've got my eye on a new manager."

The Manchester United chairman of that period, and the club's pre-war saviour, had been looking around for a man to build a new United team when the war in Europe collapsed, and he added, in whispered undertones: "I've had a sergeant-major recommended to me who used to be a top professional before the war, and I'm absolutely certain he could do a great job for the club."

The war was fading, and I was on leave from France, but when he mentioned Busby's name I was able to supply a personal assessment, having known Matt well for many years, and especially when he moved from City to Liverpool. Just then, he was largely connected with the Army's sporting activities, and surrounded by other soccer personalities such as George Hardwick, Frank Swift, Tommy Lawton, Willie Watson, Neil Franklin, Bert Sproston, Jimmy Mullen, Wally Barnes, Ted Drake, Frank Soo, Stan Matthews, Raich Carter, George Smith, Billy Elliott, Cliff Britton and Joe Mercer.

He always used to say he was a misfit in uniform, yet I think the Services did him a good turn. For they supplied extra confidence and taught leadership and how to handle men whereas when I first knew Matt he was an extremely quiet person tending rather to shyness. For example, when I included him in a series about Scottish and Irish internationals for the old Sunday *Empire News*, during his Anfield days, and Matt, Jean and I discussed his first-ever article over chipped teacups in the old Liverpool Exchange Station buffet, he had very little to say, and the quotes I wanted had to be almost dragged out of him.

Of course, his early days in the first stage of his life were sheltered while being reared in a quiet little pitman's cottage in the Lanarkshire village of Orbiston, which lies to the east of the Glasgow conurbation. He was only a nipper of six when his father was killed by a sniper in the mud of Arras, leaving Mum to look after Matt and three daughters. She pondered on the advisability of emigrating to Australia, but stayed put.

Instead of boarding the next boat, Matt, the schoolboy, entered the second stage by becoming a miner for a short time. He went down the neighbouring Orbiston Colliery for his weekly wages, but it was an experience that didn't appeal. I'll never forget him once saying to me: " I never want to try that way of earning a living again."

Weekends were spent playing for the local Orbiston Celtic, sometimes with Alec James at inside-left, and as his soccer skills developed better opportunities came around. Very soon he graduated into the third stage via Alpine Villa to Denny Hibernian, a club which has always provided a recognised hunting ground for scouts from over the border.

He always thoroughly enjoyed those days in Scottish junior soccer, and it really wasn't very surprising when one of the scouts sized him up, mailed a report to Maine Road, and Manchester City came along with an offer of £5 a week during the season, and £4 in the summer, which may not sound anything but peanuts now yet just then was a tidy wage, especially to fellows who sweated for a living under the ground.

But the going was tough in that fourth stage, because City had a wealth of inside-forwards. Finally, he was left struggling, began to feel disheartened, and wondered about the wisdom of packing his bags and going back home to the pit. He decided to hang on for a bit, and give himself a better chance.

One day, there was a call from Old Trafford. Someone from

across the way had been studying him in reserve games, and was asking questions. It's always been understood it was Rocca, but what I do know is that shortly afterwards Harold Hardman, who was the club chairman at the time of his death, watched Matt several times, and told me later they could have shaped him into first-class material in next to no time. Anyway, they tried signing him. They offered £150, and if that appears particularly small it must be remembered that the second transfer then was merely £7,000, and, secondly, Matt was only an unknown reserve. The suggestion was turned down flat. But during the conversation United told Peter Hodge, who was then City's manager, that they considered Busby was well worth persevering with as a wing-half. Peter pinned his ears back. He'd not thought of that idea. He switched Matt from inside-forward to the middle line, and he stayed at right-half for the rest of his long soccer career.

He had a great time, too, because he was with City in their golden era between the wars when they made successive visits to Wembley, and he won himself a spot in the Scottish team, though I always thought the selectors passed over him far too often. His best playing years were with City. No doubt about that. But for fate stepping in once more, he might have ended his days with the Blues. For it was really just by chance that Liverpool signed him.

A deputation headed by Walter Harrop, the Liverpool chairman who then also presided over the F.A. Challenge Cup Committee, made a special trip to Manchester to sign Alex Herd. Liverpool badly needed an extra forward of class, and thought that the nimble, ball-playing inside man would be just right for them.

Alex, father of David, the well built Scotland, Arsenal, Manchester United and Stoke City scorer, had a great game that afternoon. So they were doubly keen to get him. But the City board knew Herd's value to them, would not listen to any transfer talk, and they all went back to their seats in the directors' box. Then every member of the Merseyside contingent sat up and was impressed with a terrific second-half display by Busby, agreed a fee of £7,000 after the game, and

Sir Matt Busby, C.B.E., the inspiration behind Manchester United for over twenty-five years, whose story is told in this book

Jimmy Murphy, the never-tiring and loyal first lieutenant, whom Matt first recruited towards the end of the war in the desert

signed Matt before departing for home. It was as sudden as that. I know because I was with the Anfield party.

He moved down the newly-opened East Lancashire Road in the fifth stage of his life, and was an adopted Liverpudlian until the outbreak of hostilities in 1939. It was a hard time because three of Liverpool's stars were almost over the top. I'm referring now to "Tiny" Bradshaw, Ernie Blenkinsop, and Tom Cooper. Blenkinsop and Cooper were defenders whom England had capped nearly ten years earlier, and Bradshaw was one of the big successes in the Scottish wizards team which thrashed England at Wembley, in 1928.

When I ran across Matt during a British Army game with the French Army, at the Parc des Princes, in Paris, just after the last of the fleeing Germans had been chased out of the French capital and their foxholes near the Sacre Coeur, and into the Chateau country, he was not quite certain about the likely shape of things to come, but reckoned it rested between Manchester and Liverpool.

Liverpool, fully recognising sterling character and obvious teaching ability, wanted him to rejoin them as a coach with a five-year contract, but his life was being planned more firmly by Gibson who was being advised by a very old friend, Captain Bill Williams, sports officer of Southern Command. He had arranged for Matt, who was greatly benefiting from his period in the Services, which formed stage six of his life, to guest for Bournemouth, and they met Gibson afterwards for a friendly chat about peacetime occupations.

There were several other possibilities, for, in addition to offers from Liverpool and United, he had been invited to become manager of Ayr United, and assistant-manager of Reading. For future historians, he signed on the dotted line for United on 19th February 1945. He was in khaki at the time, ranking as a Company-Sergeant-Major-Instructor, and had to wait until the following October before taking up the job after demobilisation.

Looking back, he would no doubt contemplate with pleasure the great game he had for City in their winning Cup final of 1934, after having been on the losing side twelve months earlier. He was in his usual rôle of right-half, immediately ahead of Laurie Barnett, and no doubt remembers the rocket Barnett got from a director just before the banquet for booting a ball into the stand while under tremendous pressure in the closing minutes. They had come from behind against Portsmouth, and were leading by 2-1 when a Pompey forward slipped a short one through in a bid to bypass Barnett. Sam Cowan, the skipper, yelled: "Belt it into the stand." He did, too, knowing there was only one spare ball, and that had been lost in the crowd for the moment, and all his team mates were pleased. Yet this director actually said to him later: "Never indulge in aimless kicking of that kind again, because it can ruin a game." Perhaps difficult to believe, but perfectly true.

Stage seven began when Matt reported for his first day as manager. He immediately set a new fashion, and one which had everybody talking. He trained with the boys, talked to them during practice games, and illustrated himself exactly how he wanted the game played. Nobody had ever done that before, and some were not too keen on the idea. They thought that managers should continue sitting in their offices, and just send for players whenever they wanted to explain particular points. Maybe that had a touch of the starched collar about it, yet it is a fact that a large number of players were rather astonished at the new system.

His predecessor, Scott Duncan never took the players out into the middle for tactics talks and all that. Oh, no. Always well dressed with an impressive rose in his button hole, Duncan also sported freshly cleaned spats over well polished boots. Matt was the opposite. He wore a track suit, called them all out of the dressing-room in all kinds of weather, joined in the practice games, putting in as much effort as the rest, and occasionally halting the game to explain certain moves and the best way to use the ball. Often afterwards when all had washed and dressed he took them into a spare room under one of the stands, and explained differing systems with the aid of a marked-out pitch on a green baize board, and twenty-two metal figures. Very definitely the new boss was no stool pigeon.

It was just about the toughest start any new manager could

imagine. The Old Trafford ground had been badly blitzed in the raids, leaving them virtually homeless, and they were sharing their rivals' Maine Road pitch, while, in addition, they were more than £15,000 in the red. But the club had some first-class players available, and he shaped a winning team out of those.

He converted both Johnny Carey and Johnny Aston from inside-forwards to full-backs, and then went to Scotland and signed a " write-off "—Jimmy Delaney, an old style attacking winger who had been playing for Scotland for nearly ten years, and was reckoned to be almost over the hill by experts north of the border. It was his first signing, and it cost him £4,000. He has made dozens of others in the intervening years, but I don't think Matt ever picked up a bigger bargain because the slim, elusive Scot slotted easily into the English scene, and went on winning more international honours. He was known as " Brittle " Delaney because of having broken so many bones that insurance companies were nervous about accepting premiums.

He gave a succession of brilliant displays, and helped United win the Cup in 1948, with Johnny Morris as his inside partner on the right-wing, Jack Rowley leading the attack, Stan Pearson and Charlie Mitten forming the opposite flank. Altogether, Delaney made nearly two hundred first-team appearances, which to me has always seemed an excellent return for such a modest fee.

Busby's team of that era was an all-international one with the exception of goalkeeper Jack Crompton, right-half Johnny Anderson, and outside-left Mitten—Good old Charlie to all the fans all the time and everywhere until he branched out into management with Newcastle and had mixed luck.

Apart from that early Wembley triumph, United were mostly the bridesmaid and never the bride. For three years on the trot they finished runners-up in the battle for the championship. In 1947 Liverpool pipped them by just one point; Arsenal had them beaten in the final run-in twelve months later, while in 1949 Portsmouth proved the better stayers. But Matt has never been a type for shrugging shoulders, and saying bad luck's spoiled his plans. He went on scheming, and changing line-ups until in April of 1952 he carried off his first championship, leaving Spurs, Arsenal, Portsmouth, Bolton, Villa and Preston in the slip stream.

The three inside men—Johnnie Downie, Rowley and Pearson—accounted for 63 of the team's 85 League goals, and it is also interesting to note that Jackie Blanchflower and Roger Byrne, two of the original Babes, were just coming into the scene.

Many said it was the greatest team United ever had, though since those days a number of opinions have been changed, and I reckon the large majority would back the immediate pre-Munich line-up of Wood (or Gregg); Foulkes, Byrne; Colman, Blanchflower, Edwards; Berry, Whelan, Taylor, Charlton, Pegg. On the other hand, there are plenty favouring the one which won the European Cup in 1968. Do you remember it? Here it is : Stepney; Brennan, Dunne; Crerand, Foulkes, Stiles; Best, Kidd, Charlton, Sadler, Aston.

But we are leaping ahead too much. Let's regress, and to the immediate post-war days when the United manager was always looking around for new strength, especially in goal, a position which for some reason or another always seems to have provided him with more than a sufficiency of headaches. There were times when the club fancied Frank Swift, and I can tell you now that the famous England and Manchester City goalkeeper was in love with the idea of joining his old team mate. The City board, however, always set their face against such a move. They took the view, probably rightly, that if Frank ran into top form for United their own supporters would start playing Old Harry about him being allowed to leave.

Matt made the first move in October of 1946 as the clubs were playing alternate Saturdays at Maine Road, while Old Trafford was still having its bomb scars removed. United were ready to make a good cash offer plus a regular first-team player, and probably thought they were in with a good chance because their arch rivals were well placed for the last line of defence.

The half-whispered suggestion was turned down flat, as it also was in February 1949, when the possibility was discussed with City chairman Bob Smith. And it came to naught when Hardman raised it with Smith over a board-room drink twelve months later, at a time when Frank had suddenly gone into business in town though remaining a registered player of the City club for the next three years.

Swift possessed a pair of tremendous hands. He could quite comfortably hold a ball in one palm, and, in fact, cover one because of being able to stretch over fourteen inches. Sometimes he was a bit tight. Like when he refused to split a bill for beer, sandwiches and a taxi I had paid for in a dash for the night train home from London. But generally there couldn't be a warmer hearted person. An instance of that comes to mind in connection with a return trip from a Wembley midweek afternoon international in which he had starred. We sprinted through Euston Station, and a youngster at the ticket barrier called out: "Give us your autograph, Mister Swift." The lad was in a torn coat and shirt. He looked as if he had lived all his life in that tough, hard-up area around the railway termini. I drew Frank's attention to him, and though there were only seconds to spare he sprinted back to the barrier, scribbled in the crumpled autograph book then dashed back just ahead of the guard's whistle.

Out of the corner of my eye I saw the youngster walking slowly away. He was oblivious of everything with his eyes fixed only on his book. And no wonder. He was probably thinking about the sensation he would cause at school in the morning, because Frank, in a flash of inspiration had written this message: "Best of luck to my old pal, from Frank Swift."

Most of United's England men who toured overseas in the late forties will also remember the 1947 trip when we flew into Zurich with one of the most talented packs of any tour, yet were beaten 1-0 by a mob of Swiss part-timers on the small but very pleasant ground of the Grasshoppers' Club. Tempers became frayed nearing the end. Someone threw an old umbrella at Swift. It just missed his head. But instead of losing his temper and tossing it back, he merely bent down, picked up the lethal weapon, handed it back to the pitcher, patted him on the shoulder, and retraced his steps to goal to the accompaniment of tremendous Swiss applause, and loud cries of "Viva la Swiftee."

In the England dressing-room afterwards he told me that while handing back the umbrella he whispered in the man's ear: "If you throw this thing at me again, I'll stuff it down your bloody throat." I queried the problem of the lingo, though most Swiss have a working knowledge of English, and Frank, laughing, said: "He knew what I was saying because the blood drained from his face, he went white, and then vanished."

FOUR

Johnny Gentleman

JOHNNY CAREY, the play-anywhere star, the brilliant scoring forward who became the master defender and the perfect reader of the game in a memorable career was one of the kingpins in Busby's early building plans. The Irishman was one of a flush of aces in Matt's manipulative hand. A skipper eagerly accepting advice from the raincoated new boss of a club that was well in the red but had tremendous assets.

When the boys started chalking up one victory after another many folk became a little glib about the reasons. Some opined it was because the team had been ready made for the job. Admittedly, there was the talent available for the shaping when the new boss appeared on the scene, but I never agreed that the task was easy. Neither did any of those closely associated with the club.

Johnny was one of those in a position to know, and he always went against the view that everything was cut and dried before Matt walked in. I remember when we once discussed that particular point, he said : "There have been many managers who have taken over good squads, yet made nothing of them, whereas Matt did a first-class job of work. He had more headaches than most right at the start for the ground was in a shambles, and the team itself only in a formative shape and had to be redrafted until he fitted the last piece into the jigsaw by the signing of Jimmy Delaney."

Carey, always a great favourite with the Old Trafford crowds, began his career in the early thirties with the famous Home Farm club, and won an F.A.I. Minor Cup medal in 1936 before graduating to League of Ireland standard with southsiders St. James's Gate, at which time United's Eire man was taking careful note of the boy's progress. He stayed at Iveagh Park for only a couple of months before sailing across the channel on a one-way ticket, and wondering all along whether it would turn out a wise move.

Altogether, Carey played twenty-seven times for the Republic, nine times for the northern counties, and skippered the Rest of Europe team against Great Britain at Glasgow's Hampden Park, in May 1947, and therefore has plenty to look back upon with pride.

Yet there were also other, and equally great honours to cherish. For instance, the English soccer writers voted him the Footballer of the Year in 1949, a year after Stan Matthews had been the first one to be nominated. Then, in 1965, when he was managing both the Republic and Nottingham Forest teams, he was handed a spot in the Caltex Hall of Fame. He made a pleasing picture examining trophies with his wife, and I wondered whether he was then giving a thought to the day when Rocca signed him for United for £250, just after he had been playing a spot of Gaelic football, and if he remembered that outside-left and goal were the only positions he didn't fill during his tremendous life on the park.

I'll bet he never forgets one occasion. I'm thinking of the time when United visited Anfield. It was shortly after the war, a Wednesday afternoon fixture. Liverpool popped one into their net very early, and he didn't look too pleased about it. But a United fan who had defied danger by going into The Kop shouted out: "Never mind, Johnny, we're right behind you." Came a second goal to the Merseysiders, and the voice called out once more: "Never mind, Johnny, we're right behind you." Liverpool had a party. They laid on a third goal in the second-half. Everybody waited for The Voice. But it was silent. Instead, another, and obviously that of a Liverpool scouser, shouted out: "He's not right behind you now, Johnny, he's buggered off."

Whenever we talked, I used to think of some of the great Irish teams he had managed. Of the great fight one of them staged in a World Cup play-off with Spain, in Paris, when

Noel Cantwell was an inspired skipper, and he had been worrying over the loss of Charlie Hurley and Mick McGrath and Alan Kelly, and the joke always seemed to be on Andy McEvoy.

Matt helped him clinch his first managership at Blackburn, then, after a mixed reign at Everton, he was associated with Orient and Forest before returning to Ewood and hundreds of very old friends in that rather old-fashioned yet sincere cotton town, where many now look upon him as a father figure, willing and able to hand out advice while living a full life for football.

Anyway, he thoroughly enjoyed his stay at Old Trafford, where nobody was ever homesick because there were so many players from all the Home countries. Which reminds me of the time when the club supplied forwards to both England and Scotland for an international at Hampden—Pearson and Delaney. The English trained on the west coast where everybody was a Rangers fan and idolised Willie Waddell. One wet afternoon we popped into a local cinema in Ayr. It turned out to be a children's matinee, and the big film was a serial about a lone ranger on the prairie. When it ended, the lights went up, and the manager walked to the front of the screen. He was in evening dress, and there was an air of expectancy about the place. Without any introductory effort, he called out : " Who is the lone ranger?" And five hundred children roared back : " Willie Waddell."

Henry Cockburn was blossoming, just then. He had settled in at left-half alongside Allenby Chilton, and immediately behind Pearson and Mitten. Boyish in his enthusiasm for the game and everything connected with it he was still working in the mill five days a week when first capped. I'll never forget the occasion. It was in the 1946-47 season when the usual half-back line was formed of Phil Taylor, Neil Franklin and Billy Wright. When the F.A. announced the new shape I dashed up Oldham Road and into the Lancashire cotton town, and gave Henry the news as he came out of the works for his lunch break. He was speechless for a moment or two. His eyes shone with delight. Then, recovering lost breath, he said, quite simply : " Wait till I tell 'em at home." That was the first of a bunch of England caps, marking a great but too short career in the top flight.

Generally a quiet type of player, he rarely caused any match official a second's worry, though once he was spotlighted in a sensational finish to a " Derby " game at United's headquarters. There had been some niggling between himself and Billy Linacre, the Manchester City winger, almost throughout the match. Then, with only one minute left, referee Arthur Ellis gave marching orders to both. They had come together at the far side of the field, and when the referee went up to them, and then pointed to the exit route the players had to slowly trudge across the green acres and down the tunnel while nearly 60,000 silently watched.

When I saw them afterwards it was obvious that Linacre was shaken, but Cockburn was even more distressed. A product of local junior soccer on the north side of the city, he had played in all the club's reserve line-ups before emerging into the League team; he was an inoffensive character whose studious style and considered delivery often reminded me of Busby in his playing days.

One of the men behind the scenes whom few heard about was a pleasant type named Joe Armstrong. Matt was very fortunate recruiting him to his staff within a short while of having taken charge. They had first met when Busby was a youngster at Maine Road, and Joe was employed by City as a part-time scout who used to concentrate very largely on junior leagues in Lancashire and Cheshire. His full-time job was that of GPO engineer, but the rest of his waking hours soon proved very valuable for United, and it occasioned no surprise when, after retiring from the Post Office, he became the club's chief scout and began touring Britain in a ceaseless search for new talent.

A rather small man with twinkling eyes, he must have discovered hundreds of promising youngsters, and certainly many have developed and matured in senior soccer over the last twenty years, saving the club thousands of pounds in transfer fees. Yet although he played such an important part as a backroom boy Joe never changed. On the last day I saw him he was just the same as on the first, never needing an extra size in hats.

I often phoned the club for team news on Fridays, and sometimes if Matt was tied up with a visitor or had dashed off somewhere he would ask Joe to give me the line-ups for the next-day games, and he always said the same thing: "Here are the teams, Eric, and if you want to know anything else you'll have to get hold of the boss because he is the only one who really knows what's happening."

Looking just at big stars, Joe could claim to have discovered Nobby Stiles, Roger Byrne, Dennis Viollet, Bill Foulkes, Eddie Colman, and Bobby Charlton, and though he was still doing his stuff at seventy-six he was the only scout who stayed on right to the end of a game between Manchester and Ayrshire schoolboys which was played out in a temperature more favourable for brass monkeys.

If it was for the good of the cause, he never shirked anything, even disguising himself with the aid of a false moustache, dark glasses, and a wig, though he admitted that those aids often made him feel "a right Charlie".

It made his day whenever Matt said well done or anything like that, and I reckon that one of the greatest occasions of his life must have been when Charlton was collecting his Footballer-of-the-Year statuette from the soccer writers in 1967, and paid special praise to "Uncle Joe".

It was in that period that United began looking around for extra half-back strength, and decided that Roy Paul, of Swansea Town, would suit them very well. They contacted the South Walians, and when this plan leaked out it was given the big treatment everywhere. I remember writing a back page lead about it for the *Evening News* because my inquiries showed that United were likely to set up a new transfer fee record.

Paul, a strong-tackling wing-half and outstanding Welsh international, halted the deal by sensationally joining others in a dash to Bogota, where Neil Franklin and George Mountford had already arrived to take up first-class offers. They blazed the trail in the early summer of 1950, along with Bobby Flavell, of Hearts, and Jack Hedley, of Everton and

Charlie Mitten, but their hopes of a quick fortune out in South America collapsed like a pack of cards when F.I.F.A. announced that all Colombian clubs were going to join the international federation. It meant that those players who had not been released by British clubs would be left high and dry.

So back they came. And Manchester City, who had also been very interested in Paul, slipped quietly down to Swansea, talked quickly, and within six hours City secretary Wilf Wild was on the phone to say they'd signed Roy, and he would be making his debut three days later. In order to beat United, City had to pay £25,000. Maybe that sounds paltry these days, but then it was the highest fee any British club had ever met for a wing-half, and, in fact, the greatest fee of the early 'fifties was only the £34,000 which Sheffield Wednesday paid to Notts County for Jackie Sewell.

Everybody at Old Trafford was very disappointed because the Welshman would have done them a world of good. He was a tough dyed-in-the-wool skipper who enjoyed life and hated defeat. Whenever we discussed Wembley he always used to say : " Whenever I walk up to the Queen, I'll be skipper of a winning team." It didn't quite turn out that way, because when he led Manchester City against Newcastle United in the 1955 final, they ended up as losers. The dressing-room underneath the north stand—a grim concrete " palace "—was a shambles of naked bodies and disappointing looks when I reached it after the game. The most miserable person was the rugged Welsh star, a man who had often known it tough in his beloved valleys, but was going through his own private Hell, just then.

It was no good giving him a sympathetic pat, and murmuring the old woman's comment about there being a next time. The sweat continued tracing a zig-zag pattern down the bronzed cheeks. He started tearing off his crumpled shirt while the others hauled their tired bodies up the cold, concrete steps to the king-size sunken bath on the raised floor. He halted in his labours, wiped away some of the sweat with the back of his hand, looked across at me, and said with great feeling : " It's a devil."

Twelve months later, however, he was on top of the world. They won the Cup at Birmingham City's expense, though he had been very worried about the issue shortly before the start. For when they were halfway down the tunnel on their way to the pitch, and the 100,000 fans packed in Wembley's great bowl, he suddenly halted them, turned round, raised a clenched fist, and said: "If we don't win this time somebody's going to get a load of this afterwards."

Often, he used to wonder how he might have got on as a United player. I used to consider that score, too, and I believe he might have risen to even greater heights with such as Carey, Aston, Chilton, Delaney, Pearson, Rowley and Downie around him.

FIVE

Reluctant Goalkeeper

Over the years, Busby has scored many great successes and he may have difficulty nominating today the one he prizes best though most folk will probably pick that European Cup triumph of three years ago.

There can be no doubt, however, that his first great moment as a manager was when the team fought its way to Wembley in 1948, and won the coveted trophy at the expense of a strong, all round Blackpool outfit. They had actually set out to improve on their previous season's League record and carry off the championship. Having finished second to Liverpool in the first post-war campaign they felt capable of going one better the next winter. But, instead, they slotted in behind Arsenal while changing courses and concentrating on the Cup.

When the Third Round draw sent them to Villa Park, many could not see them making any further progress because at that time the Villans were one of the best teams in Britain, and particularly hard to beat on their own famous enclosure. Yet United, touching top form, won a high-scoring game by 6-4, beat League champions Liverpool in the next stage, and added the scalps of Charlton, Preston and Derby on their way to a Wembley date with a Blackpool line-up which included such redoubtable warriors as Eddie Shimwell, Harry Johnston, Eric Hayward, Hugh Kelly, Stan Mortensen and, of course, Stan Matthews.

Old Joe Smith, the Bolton warrior who was then in charge at Bloomfield Road, was backing his boys all the way, and looked almost brokenhearted in the dressing-room afterwards, though generously admitting the quality of United's soccer.

It had been a remarkable feat on Matt's part because you must remember they were still playing *all* their matches away from home from the start of each season to the finish. Old Trafford was not then ready for re-occupation, and, with City's continuing agreement, they played at Maine Road every other Saturday, and sometimes in midweek.

That was a tough arrangement for the Reds, but it was financially good, especially when you look at it this way. If they had played their games at Old Trafford, they couldn't possibly have got much more than 40,000 inside the ground in those days, whereas they generally had many more thousands watching them at City's headquarters.

Here's the big proving point. On 17th January 1948, United played Arsenal in a First Division game, drawing 1-1, and attracting 82,950 spectators. That stands as the all-time English League crowd record today, just rubbing out the previous top gate of 82,905 who watched a League match between Chelsea and Arsenal, at Stamford Bridge, on 12th October 1935.

They were always getting bigger crowds than City, whose directors gradually got a bit needled about it, especially when some supporters complained that the Blues were having to play on a pitch which was being kicked out of shape every week instead of having an occasional rest from first-team fixtures. I remember the terrific row that followed my announcement that City were going to tell United to quit their ground for the 1949-50 season, though they were allowed to return for the early games in the European Cup, a few years later.

Actually, United nearly missed their way in that tourney. If they had been lacking spunk like Chelsea they would have done. For the Pensioners, invited to compete after becoming English League champions in 1955, decided not to do so when both the F.A. and the League told them to stay out because extra European dates might land them in trouble in fulfilling their own domestic ones. In effect, they were told to ignore the idea, and did.

Shortly afterwards, Harold Hardman, the United chairman, told me that whenever his club got the chance they would take it and to hell with everybody. I remembered that immediately Busby's boys had won the title the following year, tossed the vital question in his lap, and Harold said: "What I told you nearly twelve months ago still stands today, and we're going to play in this European competition irrespective of what anybody might say."

Hardman, a small but wiry personality, had great command of the English language. He never looked capable of playing a strong hand, but I never doubted his strength after once watching him "slay" delegates to an annual conference of the Lancashire County F.A. in Blackpool.

Of course, Hardman had caught the germ. Like everybody else at Old Trafford. For they not only topped the League in 1956, but did it again for good measure the following year when they left Spurs trailing down the course, and, in 1957, fought their way to Wembley, and to the semi-final of the European Cup. When we once looked back and recognised how nearly his beloved United team had chalked up a fantastic triple victory, Matt pointed out that in those days he had virtually two first teams available most of the time.

Aston Villa defeated them in the F.A. Cup final of 1957, triumphing by 2-1. There was a hollow ring about it, though, because they had only managed it against opposition deprived of a first-class goalkeeper because of a sixth minute injury to Ray Wood. All the United players had felt happy about the final having clinched the league, but the outlook suddenly changed when Wood was in the wars.

Before that unfortunate period it had been a tremendous winter made additionally exciting with the introduction to some of Europe's top teams, most of whom the ordinary fans knew little or nothing about or even the towns from which they hailed. When United had finally been accepted by the overseas authorities and the first round draw was made for two-legged battles one could sense early and growing excitement, particularly in the Greater Manchester area. Yet there were those who still doubted the likely attractiveness of unknown teams from other countries. Members of the Manchester City board were among them. Chairman Bob Smith

Wilf McGuinness, the home-spun England wing-half whom fortune deserted in the hot seat

(Left) George Best, the mercurial Irishman who has won more fans and set more people talking than anybody else in the game for over a century

(Below) George Best takes on Bobby Moore, the West Ham and England skipper

didn't think the games would prove paying propositions, and said so.

The day before United lined up against Belgian champions Anderlecht at Maine Road, having beaten them 2-0 in Brussels a fortnight earlier, he said he would be turning up in decency as chairman of the club providing the ground, but he'd be surprised if there were more than ten thousand. Well, they rolled up. By the time Bob was leaving home in Whalley Range every road and street within miles of Maine Road was jammed solid with traffic, and the famous ground was almost bursting at the seams. I've not the slightest doubt that everybody who went that historic night will always remember it. United slaughtered the pride of Ghent, Antwerp, Liege and the Ardennes. They hit ten of the best home without any concession, and their winning aggregate of 12-0 included five from Dennis Viollet, four from Tommy Taylor, a couple from Bill Whelan and one from Johnny Berry.

Next came Borussia Dortmund, beaten on aggregate by 3-2, and Atletico Bilbao, who lost by 6-5, then, at last, the semi-final loomed ahead, and against such redoubtable opponents as Real Madrid, who ended up on top by 3-1 in the first leg in Madrid, and then shared four goals in a terrific tussle at Old Trafford in the closing weeks of the season

The Spaniards went on to win the trophy, and, altogether, carried it off in each of the first five successive years of the competition. Busby paid them full credit. For afterwards he said : " We were eliminated from the European Cup at the semi-final stage because we lacked the experience to match a truly great side like Real Madrid."

Remembering how many folk just shrug their shoulders and say doubles are virtually impossible and the tremendous amount who scoffed when Don Revie set his own target in the sky, it's particularly interesting to recall Matt's reaction to criticism in the fifties. He said, then : " It's been suggested that Manchester United had too much on their plate with strong bids for the League and Cup, and also the European Cup. That might have been true if we had only been on a par with other clubs so far as playing strength is concerned, but the great wealth of reserve talent at Old Trafford makes the possibility of treble success quite a reasonable proposition."

I suppose there would be an additional reason for personal satisfaction with the performance of that particular team because Matt could say it was formed of players he had coached, and gradually introduced to the game. Gone were such as Crompton, Carey, Aston, Chilton, Cockburn, Delaney, Morris, Rowley, Pearson and Mitten. Charlie had ended a fifteen-year connection with the club when he joined the Bogota club, Sante Fe, and altogether five of them had moved into managerships.

Crompton, now in his twenty-fifth year at Old Trafford, and proving a very efficient head trainer, is, perhaps, the greatest of the " old retainers ", if I might use that term. Yet he remains a quiet man behind the scenes, the reluctant goalkeeper who served the club so well for so long out on the park.

Reluctant? Well, that's what I'd say. Because in his schoolboy days he always fancied playing at either inside-forward or full-back. It was only in his final year that anybody thought of putting young Jack between the sticks, and he can't quite remember the exact circumstances even to this day. His likeliest solution is the oldest one in the book —the chap who owned the ball wanted to be an inside-forward, so he had to play where no one else wanted to play and, as usual, that was in goal.

Looking back to that time, he always says it's a bit of a mystery to him because he very definitely preferred playing up-field, and was certainly a reluctant goalkeeper in the formative years which, after the classroom door had closed upon him, led to such sporting centres as the YMCA, which has produced some really good players. Yes, top rate blokes such as Johnny Aston senior, Pearson, Anderson, Byrne and dozens more.

Like many others of that era, he graduated to Newton Heath Loco, and, later, Goslings, one of the greatest of the non-league clubs in the early war years. They were such good pot hunters that one season, believe it or not, they won absolutely everything it was possible to win, collecting no less than six trophies, and their line-up often included not only Jack but also Joe Walton, Henry Cockburn, Len Langford, Albert Mycock, Cliff Frear, and Walter Shepherd, who was an English amateur cap.

When he was persuaded to become a full-time professional and throw in his lot with United, Jack Breedon was first choice 'keeper and Crompton had the history of a broken leg which halted a career in the RAF but didn't stop him guesting for Stockport County in some games with scratch teams. It was fun, and it kept him almost match fit until United began calling on his services, and, when hostilities ceased, he was their regular No. 1 in every way.

One could say he has had a good soccer life, and is still enjoying it. But that's not been quite the case with some of the others who teamed up with him for many years. Take Rowley. He worked hard in management, but the final odds always seemed against him. Pearson was another of the unlucky ones. A fine England player in his days and a rather delicate inside-forward, he seemed set for the future when Chester offered him their managership. That great gentleman of the game, John Harris, had just moved on to take charge of Sheffield United. Stan was a very pleasant personality, and very good to everybody. Maybe too good, because unfortunately he only lasted twelve months.

They say it's the luck of the game. . . .

SIX

The Babes

THE BUSBY BABES! What a great and colourful name. A title to at once titillate and inspire, and one which gradually spread to all corners of the earth until finally paid the compliment of immitation.

It marked the fruition of youth plans which Busby had first drawn-up in the early months of his managership. But how was such an unusual name thought up? That's what many have debated, and yet there is a simple explanation. On one of the days when the United chief decided to " blood " another couple of his youngsters, it was noticed that there were to be no fewer than seven in the team whose average age didn't even reach up to eighteen!

Tom Jackson, who followed the club for the *Evening News* for many years, and was one of those who lost his life at Munich, had gone to Old Trafford for anything that was going, and was handed the team by Matt, who pointed out that the majority were teenagers. We discussed this over the phone, and when he later came on with his story it was more than ever apparent that here was a line-up liberally dotted with youngsters who had not been away from school very long. I commissioned pictures from the office library, and they just looked like a bunch of sandboys breaking away from their mothers' apron strings. They were like babies. That was it. So I wrote a streamer this way—" Busby Bloods His Babes ". The morning papers loved it. All followed the same line. The new boys became the Busby Babes, and the title stuck.

It was yet another new chapter in the history of the famous club. A new chapter which Matt had not datelined because of uncertainty about general development. It is around twenty-six years ago since he first began thinking in youth terms for United, yet I still clearly remember him enthusing about the possibilities. He wanted to avoid encounters with the bulls and bears of the transfer market as much as possible, strictly limiting the spending of hefty sums on ready-made stars, largely building his own teams from home-grown stuff. A very laudable idea though it didn't then seem to be one which might also keep them up with the pace-setters in the chase for the really big prizes.

He began to get excited, both inwardly and outwardly, however, when some began coming off the production line, and, what's more, proving themselves to be made of the right stuff and ripe for further development at the top level. In those far-off days you'd only got to mention one or two of the boys and Matt couldn't stop talking about the rest, and how they automatically insured a great future for United.

Let's glance back. Let's revive the memories of the older supporters, and at the same time, introduce today's teenage fans to some of those earliest babes. Such as Roger Byrne, Duncan Edwards, Eddie Colman, Mark Jones, Brian Birch, Albert Scanlon, Jackie Blanchflower, Ronnie Cope, Jeff White-foot, David Pegg, John Doherty, Bobby English, Johnny Giles, Shay Brennan, Dennis Viollet, Ken Morgans, Ian Greaves, Billy Whelan, Colin Webster, Geoff Bent, Freddie Goodwin, Wilf McGuinness, Bobby Charlton, Bill Foulkes, Tony Hawksworth and the rest.

It was chiefly from those that the great Youth Cup team of the early fifties was shaped until, one by one, they moved up into the League line-up as the majority of the players who had given the club such a brilliant post-war start began nearing the end of their individual careers. They had not only carried off the Cup but also been title runners-up in four out of five successive seasons before winning the championship in 1952—on the very last day of the campaign.

Arsenal, who had been breathing down their neck for some time, were the last-day visitors to Old Trafford on Saturday,

26th April, when the top of the First Division chart read like this—

	P	W	D	L	GLS F-A	PTS
Manchester United	41	22	11	8	89-52	55
Arsenal	41	21	11	9	80-56	53

The Londoners were in with a chance, even though it was only an outside chance. Victory for the Gunners would have put them level on points, but to take the honour on goal average they needed to triumph by at least seven goals. As it turned out, they didn't even score one, but, instead, United hit six without reply so there was not a shadow of doubt about the sideboard for that particular trophy. It was a wildly enthusiastic crowd which continually cheered on this team—Allen; McNulty, Aston; Carey, Chilton, Cockburn; Berry, Downie, Rowley, Pearson, Byrne.

Some managers I have known would have taken things easy after that kind of success, and simply hoped the players would stay the pace a bit longer. That kind of attitude has never been in Busby's make-up. He has always looked ahead, and planned well, which is exactly what he did in 1953, the year after that title triumph. He began breaking up his winning team.

It must have given him many sleepless nights, because he is very essentially a warm-hearted person, and pulling old friends out of the team would not be an easy task, especially when it came to explaining the move individually to the players affected. Yet he never flinched, went on gradually re-modelling, and then suddenly pulled out the old cheque book, this man who never throws money around, and almost set up a record as a spender. He paid out £29,999 to Barnsley for the privilege of taking Tommy Taylor away from Oakwell. At that time, the only other club to have paid more for a star was Sheffield Wednesday, who had given Notts County £34,000 for Jackie Sewell.

Foulkes, who only stepped down from first-team duty a couple of seasons ago, was brought in at right full-back.

Byrne switched from the wing to partner him on the left. Edwards was handed the left-half spot, Colman came in at No. 4, and Blanchflower and Jones were left to fight out the centre-half berth. Worried for some time over an ageing defence, Matt felt that this shuffle would give him the extra strength in coverage, and then faced the problems of attack.

He was lucky there because there were dozens of up-and-coming candidates knocking on the door—Pegg, Whelan, Charlton, Morgans, Scanlon, Viollett and others. All willing and ready to show their paces. All in the first flush of youth, and just waiting for the signal from the boss.

The " old boys " kept Mum, though quite obviously some of them were unhappy, just as Matt himself had sometimes been over team changes when he was with Manchester City. One of the old internationals who lost his place told me a long time afterwards : " We all felt it very much, you know, especially as we had been so successful together, yet we recognised it was anything but easy for the Boss to have to drop us, and then explain exactly why."

So there they were. Out of the first team. And the Busby Babes began battling for recognition, gradually matured, and in 1956 showed their all-round strength by walking away with the championship. That's the correct way to describe their performance. It was a one-horse race if ever such a description could be applied to the chase after the First Division's top honour. For it was almost in the bag at the turn of the year, a certainty with still a month to go, and finally left them sitting high and dry, eleven points ahead of their nearest challengers, Wolves and Blackpool. They had atoned for sensationally losing to Bristol Rovers in the Third Round of the F.A. Cup, and, for good measure, the reserves headed the Central League.

So the inevitable spotlight turned onto these kids who only averaged twenty-one, and the usual topliners vanished from the scene. Aston, who had been an England defender and must have taken tremendous delight watching his young son John climb into the team, was taken ill shortly afterwards and spent some time recuperating on the North Wales coast.

I used to write to him occasionally, and then he came back home and tried his hand at a newsagent's business until becoming one of the Old Trafford backroom boys.

I always reckoned that of the new boys Taylor was the toughest. A six-footer, he had learned the game the hard way in the South Yorkshire coalfield where they still believe that where there's muck there's brass, and a cap goes on winning preference over a soft hat. Or any other kind of head gear, for that matter. Well, Tommy first claimed attention for magnificent efforts on behalf of Barnsley Boys, and, of course, was recruited by the Oakwell brigade. No boys in that mining town would have considered signing for anybody else but the Barnsley club. Because that was their club. The one they all supported.

He took all the knocks that went his way without so much as a grumble. After all, he was nicely built to take anything. Like the rest of them in those days, in that particular part of England. He was just beginning to pick up the goals nicely when Joe Armstrong heard about him, nipped smartly over The Snake, and returned to give Matt a glowing reference. Barnsley were ready to talk turkey immediately, because their own wobbly finances needed bolstering. But the boyo himself was not too keen about moving until the United manager diplomatically explained his possibilities in a higher sphere and in a team of better players. Tommy began to see the light, and Matt purposely trimmed the fee a pound short of £30,000 so that it wouldn't look quite so big when the boy read of it.

It was March of 1953, the year of the Matthews Cup Final, and he settled in so well that he hit seven goals in his first thirteen League games. What's more, within a mere couple of months he was flying to the other side of the world with the England party, won his first cap against Chile, in Santiago on 24th May, when his early goal from inside-left set the team on its way to victory, Nat Lofthouse grabbing the second.

He also scored a bull against Uruguay, in Montevideo, seven days later—where he partnered Johnny Berry as a club left-wing—but an odd goal reverse brought changes for the final game of the South American tour, the Froggatts taking over. Yet Taylor had made his mark, was in the World Cup team the next year, though he had to wait until 1956 before making his debut in the Home international championships. He was then handed the inside-right role against Scotland, and it was the first time he had ever seen Glasgow's famous Hampden Park. The same went for Edwards, who was at left-half, just ahead of Byrne.

I always associate a special incident with that international. This way. The England team was chosen in London, one evening, then circulated by the Press Association on the morning paper service, and it made all the sports headlines next morning. One well known national writer heartily disagreed with Taylor's selection, and came down very heavily on both the selectors and the youngster.

It was such an obviously unfair pre-match comment that I decided to put the score right by producing a special piece in the boy's favour. So I went over to the training headquarters in Salford, where all the first and second team players were having a private practice game directed by the boss from the centre of the pitch. Busby walked over, obviously surprised to see me, and asked if anything was wrong. I explained my self-imposed mission, and, after saying that that particular piece had greatly annoyed him, too, he called Tommy across, and said: "Eric wants a word with you about that piece we've been talking about, and you can talk to him quite frankly because he won't let you down."

Tommy talked frankly. It was soon obvious he was deeply upset. He said he'd heard the team might be announced on the evening radio but had been out with a few friends and forgotten about it on his return to his digs. But he was up earlier than usual, and couldn't get downstairs quick enough for a peep at the morning paper. Then he added, rather slowly: "I was up in the skies one second after seeing that I had been picked, and then I came down to earth with a bump when I saw what had been written about me. I lost all my appetite, pushed the breakfast away, and went back upstairs to think on my own. I don't mind anybody belting me during a game or afterwards, but I do think people might wait until a kick-off before saying I'm a bad choice."

He went on talking in circles about the story, and when he returned to the practice Matt came over once more. I gave him the gist of Tommy's grumble, and he said : " I've already told the lad to forget it, and give 'em the right answer by going out at Hampden and playing his best."

I lined up with the overall view, and in the *Evening News* that night backed his selection all the way, gave his opinion, and then lashed some of my own journalistic friends for pieces written in haste and bad taste. It was some satisfaction a few days later when the chief culprit rang me to say that on second thoughts he realised he'd gone a bit too strong. Frankly, though Tommy was a good player I always thought that my old pre-war friend Dixie Dean was better. Taylor himself was always interested in the old school. Once he persuaded me to loan him a carbon copy of Dean's life story which I had written for the old *Sunday Empire News* many years before, and whenever our paths crossed he always brought up some odd point about Dean.

It all did him a bit of good, anyway. We were always firm friends which was probably to be expected, and my later dealings with this man who developed into England's regular leader strengthened my original opinion that he was one of the straightest and friendliest players I had ever known. Which I always told him he should be coming from the same county as myself. He always liked that crack.

Viollet, a dyed-in-the-wool babe if ever there was one, never seemed to catch the selectorial eye quite as much as Taylor, though before moving to Stoke City he had scored more than two hundred League and Cup goals for United, and was always held in high opinion by all the fans. A product of the Manchester Schools' team, like so many others in the same camp, he simply lived for nothing else but football from a very tender age, He was always friendly with David Herd, a big rival for a spot in the same attack on coming north from Arsenal, after having first signed professional forms for Stockport County while his dad Alec was playing for the Edgeley club. As boys they used to slip quietly into the Maine Road stand, sit in the semi-darkness of the back row, and quietly watch Alec, who was then with City, and all the rest of the players training on the running track below. They invariably huddled together, nipping round every time the school was on holiday.

All the time, they kept a wary eye open for the club steward's dog, a tough mixed breed which liked baring its teeth, growling, and hated all the boys, for which I could hardly blame it, especially remembering how they used to torment it at every possible opportunity though always keeping well out of range. It particularly disliked their habit of blowing raspberries. One day, four of the players joined together in a big one as they sprinted off the field and turned into the tunnel which leads to the dressing-rooms. The enraged beast leapt down the stand in record time, and had reached the dressing-room before they'd finally closed it. There were frantic calls for help as those inside kept the door jammed to with almost half the animal inside, and the rest outside. Eventually, the steward arrived, clamped a lead on, and led it away while the boys sweated it out. They never blew another raspberry.

When, some years later, both were fellow professionals at Old Trafford, Byrne often made it into a threesome, though slightly older, and having the edge in experience. Roger possessed an exceptionally good I.Q. He had fought his way into the team which won the 1952 title, having nudged Mitten out of the No. 11 spot. Ambitious to be a qualified physiotherapist when playing days were over he studied at Manchester Royal Infirmary, where he met and married a ward sister.

Along with Berry, he survived the remodelling, took over the captaincy, and was heading towards his fiftieth England cap when the Munich crash wrote Finis to a fine career. A fullback of stylish mould, often reminding me of Sam Wadsworth, of Huddersfield Town's great years, Roger once fancied himself as a sports journalist. So when he called at the office for the weekly ghosting of an article which always appeared in midweek, I thought we'd see the potential. Came a period for discussion of a subject, then I moved out of my chair and said : There's the typewriter and plenty of copy paper, so it's all yours now, Roger."

He typed a few lines, tore the paper away from the roller, then had another go and another, but finally gave up the effort, saying he'd see what kind of a start he could think up at home over the week-end. On the following Monday, when turning up in the office as usual, he rather shyly produced some pencilled notes, and said : " It's fair enough, you're a writer, I'm the footballer. In future, I'll just try and jot down a few points and not bother about the likelihood of a newspaper career for the time being, anyway."

Well balanced in all things, he idolised two people in sport—Matt and Billy Wright. Whatever the United manager said was always O.K. by him. I do believe he would have gone to the ends of the earth if Busby had asked him to do so. Whenever any remarkable switching of the team occurred and we discussed it, he always finished up by saying : " It must be right if the boss says so."

It was the same with Wright. Whenever England were on tour abroad, the England skipper and Roger were always together—training, sightseeing, present-gathering. It often seemed to me that when Billy's turn came to stand down, the Manchester United man would have been the natural successor to the England captaincy.

SEVEN

Munich

The Babes were growing up. They were winning laurels everywhere. Not only in their own country but in many others. And as they delighted in the arts and graces of the game Busby the starmaker looked back to his first big team, then thought of the new one, and said : " A few years ago I suggested that the glories of Carey's days could be recaptured by the youngsters we were then bringing along, and they have already fulfilled that optimistic forecast."

He was excited over the prospects, as any manager had a right to be, and even if I live to be a hundred I'll always remember Matt saying to me one day : " Nobody could meet a finer bunch of fellows anywhere than these United boys who are bringing such credit to the old country by not only their brilliant performances in Belgium, Germany, Spain and elsewhere, but also their great dignity and bearing off the field."

That was the other point. The factor most people missed. It was perfectly true that although the majority were lively and loved life the rules were observed, and scrapes were comparatively unknown. Which, to say the least is very unusual when you've got a bunch of young athletes together in one camp.

Matt went on directing operations from his little office alongside the main boardroom, while Bert Whalley had charge of coaching, Tom Curry, Bill Inglis and Arthur Powell organised the training, Ted Dalton was physiotherapist, Walter Crickmer secretary, and Les Olive, now in full charge of administration, was then Walter's assistant after having served as reserve team goalkeeper.

The boys became known as The Red Devils. With very good reason, too. Because they carried off the Football League championship in 1956, and then again in 1957, when they finished up as beaten finalists at Wembley, reached the semi-final of the European Cup, and won the F.A. Charity Shield. I reckon that if Ray Wood had not been injured in the sixth minute of their Cup Final with Aston Villa, United would have completed the double that particular year.

Perhaps that is just a load of supposition, as jealous viewers of the club's results might say—and did—but you've only got to remember the old theory about ten men never winning at Wembley to realise exactly how near the club was to bringing off a fantastic double with just a crowd of kids.

After that Cup Final defeat they went full out. For it was the lot that Matt Busby was after when they opened the 1957-58 campaign as the reigning champs. So you see, brother, Leeds were not the first club to have everything in their sights, and look a reasonable bet for achievement. In United's case, the idea was to adorn the boardroom sideboard with the European Cup, F.A. Cup, League Championship Shield, and the F.A. Charity Shield. A pretty good collection of silverware for anybody to admire.

Everything was going fairly well and to plan at the turn of the year and, of course, there were no worries about lack of talent to draw upon with this kind of pool—Byrne, Gregg, Wood, Foulkes, Greaves, Goodwin, Jones, Pegg, Bent, Edwards, Blanchflower, Colman, Taylor, Charlton, Whelan, Viollet, Dawson, Webster, Cope, Morgans, Berry and Scanlon.

It was a wonderful experience merely to walk into the Old Trafford ground just then, because spirits were so high. Sky high, boy. For had they not shown up well in the ordinary bread-and-butter stuff of the League, and then stepped up into European class and still maintained their aplomb? Shamrock Rovers had tasted the lash in the first round of the Champions' tournament. Then Dukla Prague had been bundled out of the second stage, and a 2-1 advantage over Red Star Belgrade had been chalked up in the home leg of the Quarter Final on 14th January. It had been a great battle. The intervening three weeks to the return fixture was largely spent debating whether the boys could consolidate, and make certain of yet another semi-final appearance.

Meanwhile, Tom Jackson, who was being booked to fly with the party to Belgrade, began losing his enthusiasm. A wartime Army sergeant, he had not flown much, and preferred travelling over the ground. One day he wondered whether I'd like to go instead, and though that could have been easily arranged I pointed out to him that it would seem peculiar if such a late change was made, and he then said, rather philosophically I thought at the time: "Well, I suppose one can only hope everything turns out all right."

There were one or two players who were also out of love with the proposed flight, but kept quiet, and everybody looked fine while boarding the Elizabethan, at Ringway airport that ill-fated first week-end of February 1958. They were in similar mood on arrival in the Jugoslavian capital. And felt better than ever on the evening of 5th February, when the sharing of six goals meant a winning aggregate of 5-4, and a passport to a semi-final with Milan. It was cold and damp next morning, but all were up fairly early, eager to return home, and feeling very good over the prospect. Busby and other older members of the party settled down quickly into their seats in the aircraft while the youngsters gossiped and joked and laughed together.

It began snowing, but all were cosy and warm inside the chartered airliner as it came down at Munich for refuelling. Busby, who had had an operation on a leg three weeks earlier was very quiet, but the majority, happy in the knowledge that the Balkans were then behind them, could hardly have been livelier, especially when the captain pushed the nose down for the landing in the German city.

The Elizabethan was cleared by the airport with the clock coming up to 1500 hours. It was snowing. Twice the crew tried to become airborne. A third attempt was planned, but the plane failed to leave the ground and crashed. Altogether, twenty-three lost their lives. They included Roger Byrne, Eddie Colman, Tommy Taylor, Duncan Edwards, Jeff Bent, Mark Jones, Liam Whelan, David Pegg, Secretary Walter Crickmer, trainer Tony Curry, coach Bert Whalley, journalists Jom Jackson, Archie Ledbrooke, Don Davies, Henry Rose, Eric Thompson, George Follows, Frank Swift and Alf Clarke, two members of the crew, and two supporters.

At the time, more were in danger of dying but, like Busby, came through largely because of the magnificent efforts of Professor Maurer and his devoted and skilled staff at the Rechts der Isar Hospital, in Munich.

The news broke in Britain with a dramatic flash message over the newspaper office teleprinters. It came out like this: Rush . . . Rush . . . Rush . . . . Plane carrying Manchester United team and officials crashed on take-off at Munich . . . many deaths feared . . . end rush message. The Chief Sub-Editor contacted the Editor-in-Chief on the house phone. He dashed into the *Evening News* editorial, and said: "Phone the publishing and machine room, and tell 'em we're going to pack the page one box on the Last Extra, then we'll break page one for the Final, and get the news desk to start phoning Munich straight away."

London office joined forces. A rewrite sub began shaping the story with a dateline. Contact was established with an official German source, and as the story gradually built up and the tragic facts became clearer the news desk arranged a special flight from Ringway for photographic and reporting coverage.

Everybody stayed late. Even those subs and reporters who normally dashed away at four o'clock for commuting trains to Blackpool, Southport, Buxton, and North Wales. Both the front and back pages were schemed again as the first names of the dead came through along with the special flash: Busby dangerously ill in hospital, survival chances regarded as poor." The switchboard became blocked with callers inquiring about different people who had been on the plane. And hopes for Busby sank lower.

Then my own desk phone rang. It was a call from Granada TV. Would I go over to their studios and say a short piece about Busby and some of the United players. I was not in that frame of mind, and said so. But the official remained persistent in his plea, and added: "We have spoken to the Manchester United chairman, Mr. Hardman, and he is willing

(Right) Bobby Charlton, the boy who just missed going down the pit and developed into a record-breaking England and World Cup star

(Below) Bobby Charlton shoots over the bar during a match against Derby County

(Left) Denis Law, the Scottish wizard and transfer headliner, who came back among his old friends from the loneliness of Italian glamour

(Right) Nobby Stiles, the friendly "assassin", and everybody's darling in the 1966 World Cup

to appear and say a few words from the club's official point of view, but only if you, as an old friend of his, will come, too." I knew just how distressed he would be, and felt I had to help him. Granada sent a car round for what turned out to be a record short visit. Only twenty minutes elapsed from the moment of arriving outside the building to leaving. Afterwards, when I left him outside his solicitor's office in Fountain Street, the United chief was in a slight maze, and said : "That was a bit rushed, wasn't it? I hardly remember anything I said."

Actually, we were met on the entrance steps, ushered quickly inside, and guided to two chairs ranged directly in front of the cameras. A young woman stepped over, sprayed our faces with a white mixture. She was followed by a young fellow who first verified identities, and then said : Mr. Hardman will speak first, then Mr. Thornton." We were temporarily blinded with light, and a soft voice from the outer darkness said : "Will you speak now, Mr. Hardman?"

He explained how the blow had hit the club and everybody connected with it, and said the full board would be meeting later that evening to draw up emergency plans because whatever else the club would go on. The whisperer said : "You're going off now, Mr. Hardman, and now it's your turn, Mr. Thornton." Yes, it was my turn for a problem piece of mixed tenses because though I was taking a quick backward look at Matt's life and praising the work he had already done at Old Trafford, I also had to remember that he was still in the land of the living, though only hanging on by a thread, just then. I seemed to hear myself talking from a distance, but it must have come out reasonably because as we were driving back Harold said : "That was a nice piece about Matt."

Murphy had not been on the plane. He had been over in Ireland, for a mid-week international, but was given the news immediately on his return on the evening of the crash. It almost turned him upside down. He was a man in a whirl. For suddenly his own little world had disintegrated. Boys he had known and coached since schooldays had gone forever. And, what's more, it looked as if the Boss, who had been a close pal for all of ten glorious years, would not be with him again.

The chairman won the club breathing space with back dating of set fixtures. Jimmy and Matt's wife, Jean, flew over to Germany, and talked with the surgeons and medical staff who were becoming slightly optimistic about his chances, though it didn't seem in those far-off days that he might count for much even if he did live. Within three days they managed to move Matt and his oxygen tent into a private ward, and there was slight yet continuing improvement.

It was around then that Jimmy felt slightly better. For while sitting by the bedside, one afternoon, the old Welsh international felt a slight tug, and noticed Matt slowly turn his head on the pillow. He bent down, and heard him quietly and softly whisper after taking a deep intake of breath : " Keep the flag flying, Jimmy, and keep things going until I get back."

United's caretaker-manager returned to Manchester, and began hurriedly rebuilding the shattered team. First, there was a quick trip to Blackpool, and the paying of £8,000 for wee Ernie Taylor, the pocket general, who had already won Cup medals with Newcastle and Blackpool. Then he bought Stan Crowther from Aston Villa for £18,000, signing him in the Queen's Hotel only a few hours before the club went back into action again.

Those two plus survivors Gregg and Foulkes were the only really experienced men in the line-up which faced Sheffield Wednesday in the Fifth Round of the F.A. Cup on Wednesday, 19th February, just thirteen days after the great tragedy. The rest were largely inexperienced reserves, and this was Murphy's first team : Gregg; Foulkes, Greaves; Goodwin, Cope, Crowther; Webster, Taylor, Dawson, Pearson, Brennan.

It had been a period of tremendous rush. The chairman asked me to edit a programme, and the printers were on my back immediately. Then he wanted some music for the occasion, and not canned stuff. Three bands were booked. It was impossible to give the printers a line-up for the programme, so we decided to leave eleven blanks and let the spectators fill them in when the team was finally announced over the tannoy system just before the kick-off.

It had been a fantastic day. Nobody seemed to be working in and around Manchester. Everybody was talking about the forthcoming game. Long before the scheduled start all roads seemed to lead to Old Trafford. There were hysterical scenes. Everybody became engulfed in a great wave of sentiment, far greater than anything I have ever experienced at any other game in over forty years of sports writing.

They cheered every time a United player touched the ball. They roared applause for every home shot, even when they were well wide of the mark. They almost yelled their heads off when United slipped into the lead, and the excitement was absolutely tremendous when the Reds finally won by 3-0, unknown Shay Brennan hitting two, and equally unknown Alex Dawson netting the other. Wednesday were never in the game with a chance.

Within another ten days they were Cup fighting once more, and, with most experts predicting a firm victory for a well-organised West Bromwich team United yet again revealed their new-found strength by forcing a replay at The Hawthorns, and winning the return at home. That was a feat which particularly pleased Charlton, who, on joining Viollet, Gregg and Foulkes on the survivors' list slammed those who had been suggesting they would be relegated.

Bobby, who had only won a first-team spot the previous season, and had not then been capped, said : " Without so much as one single new recruit we have the ability to finish in the top half of the League table, and also manage to beat quite a few more teams in the Cup, but, with one or two reinforcements we're a match for the best in the land."

They almost proved him right before the end of that particular season. For they marched on and into the semi-final to meet a Fulham team that was fighting for promotion from the Second Division with an extremely talented outfit led in great style by Johnny Haynes.

Four goals were shared at Villa Park, but " Murphy's Marvels ", as some called them, won a sizzler of a replay at Highbury. This way, if you don't remember. United took an early lead, Fulham equalised, the Reds moved in front for the second time, and the Londoners reached level terms yet again. Alex Dawson picked up a third goal for his hat-trick, and, in fact, United grabbed a fourth and looked to be coasting away when the Craven Cottagers notched a third and fought like tigers for another equaliser.

Many thought they had got it when Haynes drove for the target but was blown offside, and then, with Charlton joining the scoring list United ran out 5-3 winners, and were back at Wembly for the second successive year. It provided a reminder that Byrne, at the previous year's Cup Final banquet, had said to me when I commiserated with him over the defeat by Aston Villa : "Never mind, we'll be back next year, and make a successive appearance just like City did." Roger, unfortunately was not there to see that dream accomplished.

Everybody wanted them to win the next final. At least, everybody outside Bolton. And the Wanderers, who were to be their opponents, began getting hot under the collar about the attention paid to United both on TV, in the newspapers and magazines, and on the radio. Finally one Burnden official phoned me, and said : "Tell everybody we're the other team, just in case they think there's only one."

Murphy was driving 'em. No doubt about that. The former West Bromwich man was spending all his waking hours talking and breathing the right spirit into them. When I discussed that particular point with Viollet he said : "It just looks as if he is thinking all the time that he simply must get results to keep the club going for the sake of the boss."

The boss? Oh, yes. What of Matt, just then? He had been slowly but surely improving, pulling away from the abyss, and was brought home and handed a pair of crutches. It was suggested that he might take the field with the boys on Cup Final day, but medical opinion was against any such plan. It was recognised that he was making an almost miraculous recovery, yet the strain and tension of such a performance was considered completely inadvisable. Remember, it was only three months since Munich.

So Jimmy brought the boys down that long tunnel and

into the brilliant May sunshine, and Matt watched from a distance. During the game, however, he sat just behind his first lieutenant, and alongside his other faithful friend, Ted Dalton, the club's physiotherapist, and one of the nicest fellows to know. He could talk man's talk or win the confidence of a child as he proved when once I took my eldest daughter Brenda along to his private surgery off Albert Square. She was just a schoolgirl having trouble with a foot muscle, and was nervous and fairly highly strung. He gently probed the affected part, talking quietly all the time until she was completely free of tension.

United lost that final 2-0. Lofthouse scored both goals. And when the fans streamed away from the famous stadium most were engaged in fierce controversy about the second of Nat's brace. Busby didn't join any argument. Instead, he moved slowly down the track after the stands and terraces had emptied, turned into Bolton's dressing-room, and said to the boys : " Well done, lads. You just about deserved to win."

Now, let's concentrate on that particular goal for a few moments. Dennis Stevens, the little fellow from Worcestershire, who was wearing the No. 8 shirt, hit a terrific shot from way out on the left with Nat in the middle, and Gregg looking as if he had it well covered. But in dashed Nat. Gregg finished up with the ball in the back of the net, and the United fans said it was a foul.

How does the old Lion of Vienna view it now from this distance? Naturally, he kept out of the discussion at the time by saying nothing. In any event, it didn't make any difference to the final result because the Bolton leader had given Wanderers the lead in the first three minutes, and they had been ahead all the rest of the game. But a giant questionmark has always remained over that second goal. Well, he now admits it *was* a foul.

Looking back over thirteen long years, Nat says that at first Gregg seemed to have the ball covered—" but whether he changed his mind or was deceived by the pace I don't really know, but what I do know is that he palmed it up into the air, and, sensing a sudden chance, I was in there like a flash, and Gregg finished up in the back of the net with the ball. I expected the referee to award a free-kick against me but when he didn't I wasn't going to argue about it."

There was little time for dwelling on that Wembley defeat because the European semi-finals were coming up. Within another five days United were tackling Milan, at Old Trafford, and gaining the favourable first leg result of 2-1 with goals by Viollet and Taylor, who claimed his with a spot kick.

Off they went to northern Italy a week later, backing themselves for a place in the final of the international tournament of club champions. But the Milanese had other ideas. They hit four without reply and the aggregate in their favour was 5-2. The curtains came down on that fantastic and heartbreaking winter. The chairman, and the manager and his assistant took time off, and later gathered together once more for review of the future, and a sharing of their sorrows.

EIGHT

Outstanding

BIG SOCCER and its attendant personalities are remembered in many and differing ways in every part of the world, though mostly through the printed record, or the library shelves. The performances of one tremendous figure of the postwar era, however, are being kept fresh in the mind by another and very unusual manner.

For in a quiet corner of England which borders the southern boundaries of the Birmingham conurbation, and through which the Severn winds its unruly way to the Bristol Channel, the permanent tribute to the one-and-only Duncan Edwards, of England and Manchester United, is paid in two beautful stained glass windows of a parish church.

Generally considered to be one of the most remarkable of the Babes, this soccer product, a world star at only twenty-one, has been apportioned a prominent position in the glass decoration of the Church of St. Francis, of the Worcestershire market town of Dudley. St. George and St. Francis sit immediately above two glass representations of footballers. One is in the white strip of England, the other in the red shirt of United, his first and only professional club.

It is difficult to believe he is dead. He didn't seem to have grown up. Right to the end of that last flight he had been more of a boy, with his terrific enthusiasm for almost everything, his great zest, warmth, his fine view of life and people.

He had only just left school, and was a mere ungainly sixteen years old when taking the train north for Manchester, to settle in there with other hopefuls at Old Trafford. He quickly matured. Indeed, there was little to assimilate having already learned most of the arts and crafts of the game as

Busby knew only too well, having been appraised of his amazing possibilities some three years earlier.

At seventeen, Duncan was in the first team, contesting almost every ball with experienced First Division opponents, and, amazingly, was hallmarked future England class with a place in the national Under-23 line-up the same year. Less than twelve months later, he became a full England defender who went on developing so well that many of the experts began including him in lists of great wing-halves. For myself I conceded a place alongside such fine predecessors as Arthur Grimsdell, of Spurs, Sam Weaver (Newcastle), Wilf Copping (Leeds and Arsenal), Joe Mercer (Everton and Arsenal), Jimmy Dickinson (Portsmouth).

Taller than most of his team colleagues though just short of six feet, he had collected a drawerful of England caps, two championship medals, and an F.A. Cup runners-up medallion before his time came. It certainly seemed right on the cards that he would go on playing in the top flight for at least another ten years which would have given him the chance of joining that elite circle of stars who have made more than one hundred appearances in England shirts.

That may have been looking ahead too much, but the continuing manner in which this youngster with the strength of an ox went into the tackle, came out with the ball, and used it so well always stamped him as unique among those who have maintained high standards. Proof of this exceptional talent is available from Busby, who says that even when Edwards first joined the club as an immediate ex-schoolboy there was very little they could teach him. Murphy goes even farther. He says that the lad was the greatest of all the half-backs he has ever seen. That must be more than a few.

If it had been just an average club team for which he had played Duncan would have stood out as prominently as Blackpool tower, but it was not, and there were many others almost equally gifted. I've dealt with a handful, but one must not forget others such as Eddie Colman, the cheeky chappie from Salford, the right-half with such a deceptive waggle of the hips that he became known to the fans as snake hips;

Blanchflower, centre-half and talented brother of the more famous and talkative Danny; Pegg, the box of tricks at outside-left and one of the first wing partners for Charlton, when he came into the big scene.

Then there was Jones, constant rival to Blanchflower for the No. 5 spot, the raiding right-wing of Berry and Whelan. Foulkes and Wood, the goalkeeper who was signed from Darlington to end a crisis when both Crompton and Allen had gone down injured as a vital game with Newcastle drew near. Matt had looked around anxiously for a ready-made stand-in, and recalled seeing Ray Wood giving a fine display for the Feethams club. Off he dashed to the cold north-east on a winter's day for transfer talks that went on through the night until, at last, terms were agreed at £5,000. A goodly sum in 1949, but he felt satisfied even though the actual signing did not go through until 3 a.m., and twelve hours later the new boy was making his First Division debut against the Tynesiders before an excited Old Trafford crowd.

His life was always an exciting affair afterwards, yet, if you want one who was in the limelight far longer, and often faced many critics we'll have to introduce you to the one and only—William Foulkes. The man who used to say at one time that it wouldn't pay him to turn professional.

Of course, that was way back in the old days, long before Mr. Harold Wilson's famous gimmick about the pound in your pocket, and when Spurs had just made sensational news by paying Southampton £21,000 for an up-and-coming full-back by the name of Alfred Ramsey. The fantastic period when their neighbours and rivals Manchester City dramatically offered Denis Law £100 a week to turn his back on Italian lira was merely in the distant realms of improbability.

Life was tougher, wage packets were slimmer. Foulkes knew how many shillings made ten bob, and needed some coaxing to change a set and fairly pleasant way of life. After all, this long-limbed fellah lived among his own friendly folk in the Lancashire glass blowing town of St. Helens, where he was on a reasonably good number as an assistant to the manager of a local colliery.

That was the position when United got him in their sights.

It was the early fifties, and this six-footer of brawn, agility, and a matching brain looked particularly promising. So they decided to recruit him. But that was easier said than accomplished. Mister Foulkes was no easy capture. He loved the game, and often wondered how far he might go yet, in the same moment, a well-balanced judgment always checked those young sporting ambitions.

There were cold facts to be considered. He was picking up fifteen quid a week at the pit, which was a considerable salary for any job just then, whereas part-time soccer professionals were being handed only six in the summer, and an extra one in the winter, with the occasional bonuses as softeners. They talked it over, Matt, the manager of only a few years, and the collier who liked the weekday job and football in his spare time. Matt won. Even then, this knight of the British game had wonderful persuasive powers. Bill astonished all his close friends by deciding to give it a try.

It meant a tremendous daily schedule of extra travel, fatigue, and loss of sleep. I wonder how many of today's youngsters would maintain this kind of itinerary—5.30 a.m. rise; 7.0 a.m. working down the pit; 2.30 p.m. leaving for home and dinner; 3.45 p.m. boarding train at St. Helens Railway Station; 6.30 p.m. commencing night training at Old Trafford; 8.30 p.m. leaving for evening trip back home; 10.15 p.m. arrive back; 11.15 p.m. bed.

That is how he gradually edged into the professional side of the game, and is just one of the hundreds of big reasons why the club made last season *his* benefit season—the winter of acknowledgement, the ultimate reward for loyalty, performance, and achievement.

Looking back at the early times with Whiston Boys' Club, when inside-forwards used to bounce off him, this star of two decades is probably amazed at his own long, unbroken service in the top flight. There were many in his teenage days who said the tougher Rugby League code might be the best, but a majority backed a soccer career, and time has proved them right. For since leaving the amateur ranks for the world famous outfit in the Borough of Stretford, Foulkes has worn the England shirt, played in more than a dozen different countries, and won European, F.A. Cup and Championship medals. The lot.

The season 52-53 marked the start for this forthright no-nonsense defender who graduated at fullback before stepping up to the No. 5 spot, and played in 563 league games. Altogether, including European fixtures and F.A. Cup ties and tours he made over 650 first-team appearances. What a record!

For the collectors, here's how he built up those league figures—1952-53, 2; 53-54, 32; 54-55, 41; 55-56, 26; 56-57, 39; 57-58, 42; 58-59, 32; 59-60, 42; 60-61, 40; 61-62, 40; 62-63, 41; 63-64, 41; 64-65, 42; 65-6, 33; 66-67, 33; 67-68, 24; 68-69, 10; 69-70, 3.

He came into his own at centre-half shortly after Allenby Chilton stepped down and moved to the East coast to take over the managership of Grimsby Town. Around that time the internationals in the camp included Aston, Carey, Cockburn, Pearson and Rowley. One by one they gradually faded and he became surrounded by such new caps as Byrne, Taylor, Edwards, Viollet, Blanchflower, McGuinness, and then, later, Charlton, Stiles, Law, Crerand, Best, Sadler, Kidd and Stepney.

He was in the championship line-ups of 1956, 57, 65, and 67, the F.A. Cup finals of 1957, 58 and 63, and, of course, the European Cup battle with Benfica, at Wembley, in May 1968, when United became the first English club to carry off the coveted trophy.

What kind of a life did this remarkable man lead during those eighteen dramatic seasons? If you put that one in his lap, he'll just say, quite simply: "I lived like a hermit for donkeys' years, and my own social activities were practically nil." Which is why he really appreciates the odd round of golf, these days, as he feels freer though the new job in charge of the young professionals and apprentices is pretty demanding.

If you discuss Foulkes with his boss of these many years, Busby points to just a couple of wonderful points when he always says: "There may be other players who have made more first-team appearances, such as Jimmy Dickinson, but one should remember that Bill's career is unique because he never played out of the First Division, and when one realises that he commanded a first-team spot continually at that level for eighteen years it proves not merely an impressive feat but also an achievement in skill, fitness and dedication."

Like most well known players he had mixed experiences off the park. There were many pleasant occasions to remember afterwards, just as there were annoying ones like the days when some of the younger, and less responsible sports journalists used to write him off in " think " pieces, and then list the likely successors in the No. 5 spot.

Sometimes, when one of the daily papers ran a big story to the effect that United had been watching a current international pivot and were going to size up a bid he would become worried, seek out the Boss, and then relax once more when Matt said, as he always did : " When I think your time has come I'll tell you, and nobody else, so don't bother your head about what other folk might say."

Unlike some stars I've known in the so-called Good Old Days, Foulkes has always been a careful eater. That probably explains why today he remains a wonderful walking advertisement for looking after one's body and studying foods until the correct schedule can be drawn up. He has only eaten organically grown stuff. Won't have anything to do with artificial colouring or chemicals, and believes that all clubs should interest themselves in diets and the right kind of foods, especially for the youngsters coming into the game.

It's been a long, long trail for William Foulkes, master footballer, golfer extraordinary, survivor of Munich, and a fine sporting example to all. . . .

NINE

Jimmy The One

MURPHY MADE the finest decision of his life when he joined Matt. They were two young men at the cross-roads, at the time. The war in Europe was folding. The lights were going on again. Busby had set his course, Jimmy wasn't quite so sure.

He had been in that kind of mood several times in his lifetime. There was the occasion when as a youngster in his native Rhondda he couldn't decide whether it would be better staying home and earning a living at the coal face, or chancing his luck in football. Just then, his father, another miner who had sailed across to the Principality from the pits of Kilkenny, thought the home town would be the best town, and his mother did, too, especially as she always had dreams of him one day playing the organ at her church.

But West Bromwich Albion officials were good talkers. They gave him plenty of food for thought, and eventually James Patrick Murphy, moved over the border and into the midlands to benefit from English coaches. His old horizon which was sketched by a twopenny bus ride around the slag heaps suddenly expanded, and gradually a wide-eyed boy of fifteen developed into an international star.

His sharp, incisive tackling made him an opponent to be always remembered and respected. Once the " baby " of the Welsh team at only twenty-one, he followed the equally famous Fred Keenor as his country's skipper, and never forgets a spontaneous reference spoken by Matt. It was when they bumped into each other at Anfield, while Busby was playing for Liverpool in the pre-war days. They walked into the dressing-room together. Cooper, the England and former

Derby full-back, who had been transferred to Liverpool, greeted Matt, who said to him : " You know Spud, Tommy, and if you don't always remember you need two pairs of shin pads when you play against him."

He served in the Western Desert, got a bit fed up of chasing up and down after Rommel and his Africa Korps, and then everything changed. He admits to living the life of Riley as an NCO in charge of a Services Spares Centre, which was located in a white stucco building just beyond Hellfire Pass, Fort Capuzzo and Bug-Bug. One of his many jobs included a spot of lecturing, and one day he was handing it out to a unit when Matt and some others came along, halted, and listened. Busby, who had just been offered the United post, said to him : " If you fancy a job when you come out, just call and see me at Old Trafford, because I could fix you up with one." I reckoned he could have returned to West Bromwich, with whom he had won twenty-two caps. Everybody at The Hawthorns held him in very high regard. Fortunately for Old Trafford, he linked up with Matt, and they have sweated it out together ever since.

The majority of United players have benefited from his coaching, advice and friendliness, and I always say that if Jimmy had not been on hand Charlton might have been lost to the club. For the position was very delicate when the boy first landed at the ground, accompanied by Dad, a Northumbrian miner who was making absolutely certain that he was not going to be blinded by glamour. The two men talked. They were two men who knew what the bottom of a pit looks like, and the value of unadorned truth. Jimmy's ace was his own father. He told Charlton senior about his Dad working down the Rhondda mines, and how football had been so good to him that he was able to pull his Dad out of the pit with his savings. That swayed the whole business. When Bobby finally appeared in the room after being shown around the club, his Dad just said : " What do you want to do, son?" And Bobby replied, " I want to join Manchester United, Dad, because it's my type of club."

Naturally, Murphy, who was officially appointed assistant-manager back in 1955, has had chances of other jobs. The biggest bait was provided by Juventus, when John Charles was playing for them, and Jimmy was in charge of the Welsh team. Flying over for a Home international, John brought him the offer of managership at £20,000 a year. It must have shaken him, yet all he said was: "I'm not in the least interested."

That may sound a little hard to believe, though not after one has known both the United officials a long time, and listened to Busby's interpretation of their partnership. They came together because Matt's first thought on moving into the hot seat was that running a football club is no hit-or-miss business. He once said on that particular point: "I recognised right at the start that I would need a man whom I could trust and respect for his assessment and zeal, and I got him when I engaged Jimmy. He gives me a straight answer to every question, is never what one might call a 'Yes' man, and though we sometimes slightly disagree about the quality of different players we've never had a single row."

Of course, if it had not been so, the man might have fallen to the temptation of the lira. Or, let's whisper it, taken up a £30,000 offer from the Brazilians. But he didn't. Instead he backed his tried and tested allegiances, and is just as married to a red shirt as all the faithful Stretford Enders, though it would probably surprise most of them to know that it's not always been that way. Oh, dear, no. Once green and gold were favoured, and again blue was a dominant colour. Unlike some clubs, United have never hesitated about changing. According to my records, they first sported green and gold shirts, and then white shirts with all-blue pants. The first red shirt was introduced in 1902, followed by red Vs on white backgrounds, and then we had cherry hoops before finally sticking on all-red shirts in 1934.

Hardman, chairman for seven exciting years, was never in love with the colour switching, and it was principally due to him that everything stayed red at last. Another always in favour of that colour was Walter Crickmer, who had served the club for just over thirty-eight years when he lost his life on the Elizabethan. He had watched the early teams as a schoolboy, and the day after he handed in all his books and closed that era he cycled over to the ground, and asked to see the manager, who in those years was Jack Robson, the very first man to fill that post.

Relating that experience one day, Walter, a quiet, friendly, and unassuming character said : " There was I, well scrubbed with polished boots, waiting just outside the office door when suddenly a rather fierce looking man appeared and bellowed out : " Are you the lad who wants to see me?" I muttered that I was and he took me inside, looked me up and down, asked me my name, and I said it was Walter Raymond Crickmer. He looked at me very hard, and then said I'd do but they didn't fancy folk with too many Christian names, and I'd just be known as Walter." Which he always was. In fact, dozens of people have phoned me for his surname when they've been writing to him.

He was secretary from 1926, and was generally voted one of the best any club ever had. He was never caught out for tickets on big match days. Occasionally, when additional visiting newspapermen arrived I contacted him for late arrangements, and he was always somehow able to meet those requests. Just as he was when F.A., League and club officials suddenly descended on the ground without having notified their intention. Apparently, he always retained at least a dozen stand tickets for emergencies.

When Herbert Bamlett quit the managership in 1931, Walter carried on the dual job of secretary-manager until Scott Duncan arrived the following year, and when the latter moved to Ipswich in 1937, he did the double act once again until Matt took over in 1945. Now, Leslie Olive, whom I remember as a reserve team goalkeeper in the fifties, is in charge having been promoted from assistant to full secretary in May of 1958, and he has become equally efficient.

The crash threw a tremendous amount of work on the shoulders of young Les, a very young man, then, whose bright, clean-shaven face tended to trim his tender years until he almost seemed a teenager. Yet Hardman handed him the administrative reins, and told me he felt Les could grow with the club as it was rebuilt, and that is exactly what has

Pat Crerand, tough wing-half product of Glasgow Celtic, and a bargain buy at £56,000 in 1963

Willie Morgan (left), £100,000 surprise signing from Burnley, who found the early going hard before establishing himself

(Left) Ian Ure, once a pillar in the Arsenal defence, who had to fight hard for a spot in the half-back line

(Right) John Aston of the famous soccer family, a winger with the right background

happened. Which is good for everybody and everything associated with a big club because so many hundreds of things depend on a secretary who remains friendly and refuses to panic while getting on with the job.

Hardman was of similar make-up in both his business life and the chairmanship of the club. He had three loves—home, business, football. Sometimes they changed priorities. Like they did immediately after Munich, when he worked like a trojan on behalf of his beloved club, and one of the brighter moments of that year was the fact that the financial position was good.

They had had tremendous crowds right through the winter, both before and after the crash. It was pretty obvious that a nice profit would be on the way. Yet when he showed me a rough proof of the balance sheet in his office, I was staggered The club had made just over £100,000. It was the first time that any British soccer club had gone into six figures on the right side.

His middle name should have been *Pride.* I mean pride for his club. For example, often he used to stand at the entrance to the main board-room, having the odd word with different people as they went in for a spot of refreshment. He always used to say to me: "Welcome to the other club, Eric, and now we'll show you how we entertain our guests."

Once he stripped a fellow director very quietly and efficiently, reminding me of the day another chairman did exactly the same. That time it was Alan Douglas of Manchester City, who became annoyed with the pantomime of a new director running up and down a station platform to make certain all the players were aboard. Alan said: "Watch me take this chap down a peg or two." When the chap got into our reserved compartment, Alan said to him without any preamble whatsoever: "Never again be such an idiot because it's the manager's job to see everybody is on the train, and if somebody misses it I'll deal with the manager afterwards."

Hardman's epitaph could have been borrowed from the words he said to Murphy on the morning after Munich—"We've got to keep the club going because Manchester

United is bigger than any of us." And, similarly, the epitaph for Jimmy, when his time comes, could be this: "He kept the club going in its darkest hour." That's exactly what he did, too, though at the time there was some early criticism of his quick-fire signings. Especially the buying of Taylor. Because many considered that little Ernie was "over the top", and shook their heads sadly on hearing that the reserves who were being introduced into the first team were calling him "Uncle Ernie". But if ever a player proved full value for his fee that player was Taylor, a greathearted Tom Thumb of soccer. Another Bobby Collins, if you can see the parallel. For he not only played all out all the time, but gave tremendous assistance to youngsters such as Greaves, Pearson and Brennan, all of whom had been pulled out of "The Stiffs".

Greaves, now manager of Huddersfield Town, was not even a recognised reserve yet was handed the left-back spot. Pearson was the club's third choice right-winger, playing inside to left-winger Brennan, who had been suddenly promoted from "A" team right-back. They all developed well, but just then were mere kids who, nevertheless, felt the importance of the occasion. Whenever Brennan, later a Republic of Ireland star, looks back he says that the most memorable moment of his life was when Murphy called him on one side during a training spin shortly before the first game after the disaster, and said he'd been picked for the No. 11 berth—"it's impossible to describe how I felt because I hadn't thought there would be a chance, and none of the newspaper columnists had tipped me to be in the team, but when Jimmy told me I just dashed to a phone to break the news to Dad straight away."

Brennan always reminded me, somehow or other, of the time when we flew for a game in Dublin while all the soccer pitches in England were victims of the Great Freeze. After the match Eirean officials entertained us royally. We drank Irish chasers—Irish whisky nips followed down by Guinness. Lovely. The treat went round and round until most folk in the Committee Room had had four or five. Or more. Then the dispenser, thinking of the starting time for dinner in The

Gresham Hotel, in O'Connell Street, said: "Let's just have another chaser, and we'll go."

He glanced over towards a friendly old Roman Catholic Father in the corner, who had been quietly enjoying the sociability with the rest, and asked: "Will you be after another little chaser, Father?" And the priest replied: "I will, indeed, though I'll be after having the chaser without the Guinness, this time, if you don't mind."

At Old Trafford, it was Opportunity Time for everybody. One who battled particularly hard for recognition was an old favourite of mine, Alex Dawson, the nicely-built Scot whom the fans tagged in friendly fashion—The Black Prince. He might have been a stayer with the Reds if his luck had held, but it didn't because Busby bought David Herd from Arsenal in July 1961, paying £35,000 for the privilege. His entry automatically meant curtains for Dawson, who moved on to Preston for the next six years, then had spells with Bury and Brighton before being loaned to Brentford last season. Altogether, he hit well over 200 League goals, and, being slightly sadistically inclined when it comes to soccer, I always enjoyed his battles with opposing defences. They all knew they'd been in a game at the end of a ninety-minute argument with Dawson, a man who would have delighted old-timers like George Camsell, Ted Drake, and many others. He had a challenging style, plenty of ability, and was particularly good in the air.

Yet another who shone brightly for an entertaining while was the highly intelligent Warren Bradley, presently headmaster of the Lostock Secondary Modern School, Stretford, the same borough in which the United ground is situated. It's the busy industrial town's largest state school, catering for almost 800 boys and girls, and is run to a fine schedule by Bradley and a staff of forty-eight.

There was always the prospect of a soccer career because of additional ability in the feet, but he concentrated on an educational future, and gained a B.A. in geography and history and a diploma of education while studying at Durham University, and meeting his future wife Margaret. Came a short term commission in the R.A.F., an eventual posting to the north-east, a drawerful of international caps and many exciting games with Bishop Auckland until he volunteered to help United out of a spot, and became a part-time professional.

It was always rather surprising that he moved to Old Trafford, because an earlier incident had slightly upset him, and very much annoyed his father. It concerned schoolboy days, when Bolton Wanderers were giving him the old once over, and didn't seem too interested. Bradley senior had other ideas, and Warren was invited to a United trial. It was not one of those affairs where just a dozen or so are pitched in against an "A" team, or anything like that. There were nearly a hundred youngsters milling around the place, all waiting to be called onto the pitch. They went on in couples, were watched for ten minutes or so, and then called off so that others could have a go. But when the final whistle went, and officials began sorting things out before going home, the Bradley boy was still waiting his turn. That so annoyed Dad, that he said: "You're never going to play for Manchester United."

He was proved wrong, of course, though it didn't seem as if he would be at that particular time. Another interesting sidelight on this story is the fact that his debut in the first team was against—you've guessed it!—Bolton Wanderers. Promotion was rapid. Within a mere few months he was playing for England against Italy, at Wembley and it's especially interesting to also recall the forward line—Bradley, Broadbent (Wolves), Charlton (Manchester United), Haynes (Fulham), Holden (Bolton Wanderers). Bradley and Charlton notched the goals in a 2-2 draw, and then, after Norman Deeley, of Wolves, had edged him out of the right-wing berth Warren returned for the South African tour of 1959, playing against the Mexicans in Mexico City, and the Americans in Los Angeles, when the goals that counted in an 8-1 triumph were obtained by Charlton (3), Flowers (2), Bradley, Haynes, and Kevan, the big fellow who learned the game in Bradford, developed with West Bromwich, and later starred with Manchester City.

He once said that playing in front of crowds of 60,000 or

more is always an exhilarating experience, but his success in the game never infatuated him because all the time he was set on a teaching career. So, gradually, football which had once dictated his venue of employment, became relegated to a very definite second place. The shape of things to come became clearer when he moved to Bury and mixed football with teaching geography at the town's famous Derby School. Then there was an appointment at Great Stone Secondary School until reaching a deputy headship at Denton's Two Trees Secondary School, and the top post at Whitworth Comprehensive before being offered the job of his life at Lostock.

You might think the soccer highlights of his career would be the occasions when playing in the full England team. But I don't think so. If you talk to him he provides the clue by often referring to his amateur days with The Bishops, and those successive years when they carried off the Amateur Cup. In 1955 it was at the expense of Hendon, and he was not in the line-up, but he was when they triumphed against Corinthian Casuals twelve months later, and again when they beat Wycombe Wanderers in 1957. The outstanding pleasure was the moment when he gave his Cup medal to his father.

TEN

'Ahr Albert

THE OLD place hardly looked the same when Matt returned to take over again just before the opening of the 1958-59 campaign, but he got down to all the problems though it was obvious to anyone that he was a long way short of being fit. Even fifty per cent fit.

Granted, the tough and dedicated man began turning up at the ground each morning during the week. And many afternoons, too. But the old eager step had not returned, and he tired rather easily, though never admitting such a weakness. His injured back was still paining, and he had trouble finding relief. Long trips by car and train meant a constant shifting of positions. Yet he struggled on without complaining, and was always endeavouring to exercise the limbs while looking forward to the time when he would be able to walk without artificial supports. The narrow corridor linking the boardrooms, lounge and main staircase to his own private office often provided the perfect small exercise area.

Once, when I called for a midweek chat, he was standing by the wall, had leaned the crutches against the desk, and was moving slowly along without their help. The sweat was coursing down his cheeks. Yet he was happy in the knowledge that it was the best way of regaining broken health. One had to admire the courage and optimism, though it rather startled me when he said, some time later, that he was going on the club's summer tour of America. And he did.

Many of the club officials and older players wondered whether it might be possible to pick up the threads again. One of those was Crompton. He had moved south to become trainer of Luton Town, but came back to help rebuild, and was amazed at the energy and confidence of The Boss as a new team was gradually shaped out of the transfer market to give the youngsters time to catch up.

The one that had been hurriedly lined up from the ashes of Munich chased the next championship, and, amazingly, almost took the title. It was a neck-and-neck contest with Wolves who, in the final lap of 1959, won the prize against the challenge of United, Arsenal, Bolton and West Bromwich. The regular performers of that particular era were Goodwin, Gregg, Charlton, Cope, Foulkes, Greaves, McGuinness, Viollet, Scanlon, Bradley, Carolan, Quixall, Crowther and Ernie Taylor. An amazing collection by any measurement, and one which was quickly lengthened by the addition of Morgans, Pearson, Webster, Wood, Brennan, Dawson, Haydock, English, Shields, Gaskell and Jimmy Elms.

They were difficult times. Everybody expected success all the way again while Busby began developing the young side. He kept everything in strict perspective, continually marking the priorities, and I cannot remember ever seeing him in a moment of despair, or a moment of bad temper. He sometimes withdrew himself into a mood of terrific determination, but never lost control. And he proved he was still a good operator in a buyers' market by slipping quietly past all the rest of the queue and signing Albert Quixall. That was in September 1958, just over seven months after Munich, and the £45,000 which was handed to Sheffield Wednesday, made " 'Ahr Albert ", as he was called by all Hillsborough fans, the top priced inside-forward in Britain.

It's not generally known, yet it's a fact that this smart moving England inside man almost went to Old Trafford for nothing! Bert Whalley, the coach who was lost in the crash, was holidaying at Bridlington when he noticed a youngster playing around with a ball on the sands, and revealing all the signs of latent talent. He said to the boy, who was Quixall : " Do you like playing football very much?" Albert said he did, and Bert followed up by saying : " If you'd like to join a big club I think I might be able to fix you up." But he got no further, because young Albert said : " I'm sorry, sir, but I've just signed on for my favourite club, Sheffield Wednesday."

Quixall made rapid strides with his intelligent approach to the game and an inborn ability to move into the open spaces at the right time, allied to first rate finishing power. Arsenal, Aston Villa, and Huddersfield Town were very annoyed about missing him. Yet he had been displaying the arts and graces of the game a long time. For seven years at least. It was in 1951 that he first pulled Wednesday's famous blue-and-white striped shirt over his flaxen hairs. In the interim he made over 270 first-team appearances and hit over 70 goals for the Yorkshiremen, and, in addition, played five times for England.

Regarded as one of the best forwards in British soccer of that particular decade, he was in the England party which undertook the disastrous Continental tour of the summer of 1955, when France upset all the odds by beating us at the Colombes Stadium, in Paris, and, after Spain had managed a draw, a Portuguese team nobody fancied split England down the middle for a sensational though deserved 3-1 triumph. It shook the fans back home just as much as it did all of us out there. Not a victory in sight, yet, in addition to Quixall the pool included such as Bert Williams, Ron Flowers, Roger Byrne, Billy Wright, Duncan Edwards, Stan Matthews, Nat Lofthouse, Don Revie, Jim Dickinson, Roy Bentley and Dennis Wilshaw. Obviously a sufficiency of world-class talent. Just a shortage of the right results. It remained an unsolved mystery.

The Portuguese really went to town after that unexpected victory at Oporto, the great port centre up the coast from the capital. It was the first time in four post-war internationals in their own country that they had finished on the right side. They were also still smarting over that 10-0 drubbing England had inflicted on their previous visit. I well remember the fiasco of the banquet in Lisbon, in the evening. There were fifteen empty chairs because the team and reserves had refused to attend for large helpings of humble pie.

Well, Albert, who had by then married and settled down within the proverbial stone's throw of the Hillsborough ground, was willing to stay in that industrial corner of Yorkshire for the rest of his life. But he came up against Rabbie Burns' lines about the best laid schemes o' mice and men. His own plans went for a Burton, and he transported his home over The Snake, and along to one of United's comfortable clubhouses in the southern suburbs of Greater Manchester.

How did he feel about all that? How did an honest and friendly Tyke go about his ordinary business, and try to forget that suddenly he had become the most expensive piece of football sorcery Britain had ever known? When we discussed those questions he ran his hands through his mop of hair and then said he fought hard to try and forget it, but, like others before, found that things didn't work out that way.

Once, when pressed to explain his feelings about the first few months he said, in that warm, Yorkshire dialect I always understood, but many others had difficulty translating: "I first tried concentrating on doing everything correctly so that the crowd wouldn't begin getting at me, and saying I wasn't worth the money, and things like that, but it's easy planning, and usually altogether different when it comes to the actual thing. I found myself struggling through the first month, at a time when the entire team was struggling, too, so I realised something would have to be done, though The Boss had assured me that he wouldn't worry if it took me as long as six months to discover my best form. But I worried, and began wondering whether United's slump was due to my poor displays and finally, I decided to just go out on the park and play my normal game, and absolutely forget about the transfer fee.

"By then I was familiar with the club's tactics and style, and, quite suddenly, the team hit the right blend and never looked back, climbing steadily away from the wrong end of the chart until they were challenging Wolves for the championship and then I felt a lot better."

Yet the next five years were as mixed as Heinz Varieties for the Golden Boy. There were poor League seasons but a winning Cup run, and always plenty to talk about when we met for ghosting his weekly article for the Manchester *Evening*

News, a pleasant task I also carried out for Barrie Betts, when he was skippering City. It was a joint Monday afternoon job with appointment in a quiet town centre bar nobody frequented at mid-day.

The clerks were afraid to visit the place in case their bosses saw them having the odd one, and the bosses dare not take their secretaries there because of the possibility of the clerks turning up. At least, that's how the licensee of those days explained away the lack of customers. It suited us. We wanted peace and quiet away from autograph hunters and the like. Quix usually arrived first. An hour or so later the great little inside-forward former England team manager Walter Winterbottom rated so highly, would depart, and Barrie would report, and we'd often natter to a four o'clock finish in a tea shop.

Both were good talkers, but careful. Albert would walk in, ring for a waitress, order himself a bitter lemon, and me a pinta—not milk !—and say " Got any ideas?" He got into the system of enjoying himself shooting down all mine until one day I said : " Look here, Albert, you're getting the money not me, so you'd better start earning it, because I'm becoming fed up of supplying ideas and watching you kill 'em." That pierced his armour. He looked at me carefully, and said : " Don't get upset, and we'll talk about anything you want to talk about, you know."

One day he was really turned upside down. All the boys were getting ready to leave for home and lunch after a morning training session at Old Trafford. Somebody from the General Office came into the dressing-room to say that the Boss wanted a word with him before he left. One of the players said, jokingly : " The boss is going to give you one of the top jobs, Albert." But 'Ahr Albert couldn't understand why his presence was required upstairs. He went, tapped the manager's door, entered, and was even more surprised when Matt asked him to sit down for a moment.

Then he guessed the reason. Busby, tracing a way back over recent disappointments, though it might be best if he had a rest, and so he would not be in the first team the next day. Albert had never considered such a possibility. He had never thought he would be dropped. The news really shattered him. He staggered out of the office, and told me afterwards that when he reached home he didn't know who was more upset, himself or his wife. The baby was crying, his wife spilt some gravy, and altogether it was the most miserable time he had ever known in all his sporting life.

Always a warm-hearted personality, he showed up splendidly, one day, when United were preparing for a Cup Final. The ticket scramble had been ferocious, and it was twelve days short of Wembley. Betts, turning up first for the ghosting by way of a change, mentioned that he would have liked a couple of tickets, but hadn't seen any. I suggested that he should mention it to Quix, and try his luck, but he shied away from that suggestion. Then the man himself arrived. I waded in. I said : " I know the ticket business is shocking Albert, but I've heard of a deserving cause, and it's not me, but somebody else and he's a fellow Yorkshireman." He picked up the clue, turned to Barrie, and said : " I can't do much, but if two will help I'll let you have them, and do a bit more sorting out on my own little list."

He made almost 180 appearances for United, scoring nearly seventy goals, before moving on to Oldham Athletic and calling it a day with Stockport County, gave every club good value, and was just as bright and jovial in lower grade soccer as he was in the top circle. For example : one night a friend and I went over to Boundary Park for a look-see at Oldham, and, having misjudged the kick-off time, we had an hour to spare for a gossip in an empty press box. Quix, on his way to the dressing-room, peeped in, was staggered to see me, and wisecracked on the instant : " What on earth brings Lord Thornton to Oldham? Now I'll really have to play well." Altogether, 'Ahr Albert, golden boy of the fifties, had played in more than 500 games and scored more than 160 goals for England and four League clubs before deciding to quit the scene—leaving the fans and the game the losers.

One of the best line-ups for Quix was the one which won United the F.A. Cup in 1963. Here it was—Gaskell; Dunne, Cantwell; Crerand, Foulkes, Setters; Giles, Quixall, Herd, Law, Charlton. That kind of team would very adequately satisfy most managers, but I don't think Busby was quite happy about it. In fact, he rarely said much about the early teams after the crash, though as one who knew him well and over a long period I guessed he recognised that even though they went on to win the cup the team was really not quite good enough, and, anyway, was largely a bought team.

That may seem a remarkable suggestion, especially after the boys had scored no less than fifteen goals in winning the trophy, and disposed of Huddersfield Town, Aston Villa, Chelsea, Coventry City, Southampton, and Leicester City. It must never be forgotten, however, that a winning Cup team is not necessarily a great one. That factor was fully proved by the League table. United had had a disastrous run in the ordinary bread-and-butter games. They had only just escaped relegation, finishing fourth from the foot of the First Division, just above Birmingham City, Manchester City, and Leyton Orient, and it was apparent that the defence had to carry considerable blame for such an unfortunate state of affairs having conceded 81 goals. Burnley, Blackburn, Bolton, Spurs, and West Bromwich had all thrashed them.

Anyway, Matt began his remodelling. Johnny Giles was sold to Leeds United for £32,000, and must now be considered one of Don Revie's earliest and best bargain buys. A great little man, and one of those who make the Elland Road outfit tick, these days. Disarming with that wonderful chorister-boy smile he is equally interesting on or off the park, and I'd never tire of hearing him sing so softly and appealingly—"How can you buy Killarney?". I don't know the answer to that one, Johnny, but I do know that he never quite lined up with the Manchester aces like Law, Charlton, Viollet, and Quixall, yet later became a wonderful star in his own right with Leeds.

There was quite an Irish touch about Old Trafford in those hectic years of striving to reach another pinnacle. Gregg was another English soccer had recruited as a youngster from Dublin's famous Home Farm outfit. Barry Smith had come from Londonderry, Joe Carolan from County Derry. Many others have also crossed the St. George's Channel in the intervening years until I'm thinking what a kind, warm welcome there must be an' all in most parlours for anybody connected with this particular club.

My many friends in the Republic always used to bring out the odd bottle of Irish Redbreast whenever we met over there, and I got to imagining it was due to me personality until someone brought me down to earth by saying it was surely because I came to them from the city of Manchester United!

ELEVEN

Noel, me Boy!

Noel Cantwell has done a great job for Coventry, learning the intricacies of managership as he went along, and developing assuredly into one of the really great bosses of this decade.

That's not a balloon. This Irishman knows the business on the field, and he'll very soon match up with the best off it. For he's a good learner. Never forget that. There is nothing slap dash in the make up of this extremely pleasant and dedicated personality from the ancient city of Cork.

He comes into this story now to emphasise that some years ago, as at present, the club had become worried over defensive problems. Too many vital goals were being handed to the opposition. Which, after all, was the big reason why Sheffield Wednesday tossed them out of the Cup in the fifth round of 1960. Indeed, it's a poor but truthful thought that only four First Division teams conceded more than the Reds that particular winter.

So it was hardly surprising that Old Trafford called for special reports on classy defenders, and once more Matt began thinking about an athletic six-footer who had never failed to impress in games with West Ham United. He said to Murphy : " Have another look at this feller Cantwell, Jimmy, and tell me if you think he might be the answer for us." He looked. He liked what he saw on a wintry afternoon when the majority of folk who could please themselves were sitting with their knees drawn up to their chins in front of good fires. The question about Noel's future was then raised with the people who live around Forest Gate, but there was little joy. The Hammers needed the youngster themselves, as Malcolm Allison will always tell you. Allison? Yes, brother. The one half of the Mercer-Allison partnership which has given Manchester City a drawerful of honours, was then slogging it out with Noel and the rest at Upton Park.

Persistency and the necessary cash eventually worked the oracle, as it usually does, and it became styled a gilt-edged transaction. Because he cost only £29,500 at a time when more than a dozen others had cost more though, for a brief period, the fee was the highest paid for a full-back. Actually he was pegged down to seventeenth on the transfer trail. Considerably more money had then been spent on Denis Law, George Eastham, Albert Quixall, Mel Charles. Ian St. John, Jackie Sewell, Trevor Ford, Danny Blanchflower, Dave MacKay, Phil Woosnam, Tommy Taylor, Cliff Jones, John McGrath, Alex Young, George Herd, and John McLeod. That was the quality of the circle of which he had become a member. An illustrious one, too, as the next few years fully proved.

It was a challenge moving north from East London. He knew there was already an abundance of talent on the club's massive payroll, though, as always, Cantwell was supremely confident of his own ability, and, in fact, rather relished the prospect of a fight for a first-team spot which had been almost his automatic right for some time at West Ham. Once he had reported, joined the rest in early training sessions at The Cliffe, and then gone into all-out private practice games he also knew that others were out there fighting for the glory spots, and it had become a tough business. They weren't kids larking around on the sands, or on spare bits of land. Not a bit. Most were experienced professionals who had earlier sweated out time in The Stiffs, and were none too keen to have the doubtful pleasure of additional runs.

It all totted up into just about the biggest challenge he had ever faced up to that year of grace of 1960. He wondered if it was going to be a year of grace for him as he noted some of his rivals who were similarly engaged in the grim business of fighting for six places—Gaskell, Gregg, Briggs, Foulkes, Brennan, Dunne, Setters, Stiles, Cope, Haydock, and Lawton. Yet he forced his way into the line-up while always maintaining a reasonably happy view of life.

He always took everything calmly and in measured stride.

I've never seen Noel annoyed. For a period he came onto my " ghosting " list of famous stars, and was one of the easiest fellows it has even been my task to help shape an article. He had ideas in abundance, was ever ready to examine suggestions and their possibilities, and could talk better than ninety-nine per cent of players. I would say that he and Don Revie were outstanding for analytical viewpoints and almost a matching facility for the right expressions and phrasing. Let's be truthful. Most players have their brains in their feet, and it's a helluva job dragging opinions out of them.

This was the drill with Noel. We usually fixed a Tuesday date, arranged a time convenient to Matt, and then I popped over to the ground. We sat in the empty press box surrounded by silent and deserted stands and then, after a chin wag, I would sit back and take a shorthand note of the fellow talking in his lovely soft Irish brogue, just occasionally checking if he wandered too far from the subject, I returned to the office, transcribed the notes, and the article was generally O.K. after a little bit of dressing and tightening. Off went a carbon in the night post, and around mid-day next day Noel's voice would come pleasantly over the phone : " Now, I'll be thinking that's a very good article isn't it, Eric, me boy?"

The United fans never made Cantwell their King, as they did Denis Law, and they never worshipped him quite as much as they did George Best. But everybody held him in the highest regard, and as the playing years began to end it was obvious that he was a manager in the making, if ever there was one. And when a rather fantastic mix-up ended with him being appointed successor to Jimmy Hill as chief of Coventry City the way ahead was clear, though it was obvious it would be a heartbreak route until he had rebuilt the team.

For quite a period, Cantwell vanished from the news, no doubt fully immersed in a new job and its demands. I was glad to note, however, that he proved a good man in the market when the situation called for quick moves. Several clubs shared warm admiration for Wilf Smith, the England Under-23 defender, but Sheffield Wednesday were holding tight. United, Spurs and Southampton were all out on the trail. Quite Suddenly, Noel moved in over a holiday period when most clubs forget transfer possibilities and concentrated on the fixture rush, instead. And he landed the boy at the cost of £100,000, which shows he is not afraid of handling the big money.

Well, that's Noel. Next comes Jimmy Nicholson, because for some obscure reason I always seem to pair these two names, though the present skipper of Huddersfield Town was not of his age group, and, again, is not a Man of Eire, hailing from the six counties. But they often played in the same club team.

Jimmy, one of the quiet players, didn't have to wait long for his memorable moments. He was only a stripling of seventeen when playing against Real Madrid. The Spaniards were then at their greatest, having won the European Cup five times in succession, and included in their ranks such greats as Puskas, Di Stefano, Gento and Santamaria. What's more, within a mere few months he was winning his first full Irish cap against England at Wembley, and he always says, on referring to that game, that the first experience of playing alongside such as Danny Blanchflower, Billy Bingham and Jimmy McIlroy is one that will remain with him forever.

When he moved over the Pennines to the Heavy Woollen centre of Huddersfield, where a spade's a spade and the tripe lovers say that cows born i't South have no belly linings, he was among friends from the start because the club coaches were two old United players—Ian Greaves, now the boss, and Henry Cockburn.

Now, Jimmy, a real footballing son of Belfast, has collected a drawerful of Irish caps, and retains extremely warm memories of those days with United when team switches seemed to be the order of the day and players with the middle name of Versatility often did best. It was so difficult keeping check on all the moves that one day a colleague wondered about the likelihood of this remodelling spreading to other branches of life, and instanced David Coleman having to listen to the answers to his own questions!

You'll remember my point about the massing of the Irishmen at Old Trafford? Well, the clique was very soon further strengthened by the inclusion of Ronnie Briggs, Tony Dunne, Sam McMillan, and so on. Some of them didn't stay long, reminding me of a favourite few lines from Omar Khayyám's *Rubâiyát*—"You know how little time we have to stay, and, once departed, may return no more."

It may be further commented upon that there was a trio of them in the winning Cup line-up of 1963—Dunne, Cantwell and Giles. But, if nationalities were being debated, it would also have to be mentioned that another three came south from over the border—Crerand, Herd, and Law.

Crerand is one of those Scottish stars who slipped in and out of the big news year in and year out. First claiming prominence with Glasgow Celtic, he moved into the international scene when the Scots, having been clobbered 9-3 by the auld enemy at Wembley, decided to remodel the half-back line. Out went Dave MacKay, who was then with Spurs, and Motherwell's Bert McCann, and in came Crerand and Jim Baxter, who was then with Rangers.

Pat, who made his Scottish debut against Eire, at Dalymount, in his country's World Cup team of 1961, will never be forgotten by the Irish fans because of his ruthless tackling, precise marking, and general distribution. Yet I would say he had a greater day at the expense of England, at Hampden, when handed the job of marking the visiting skipper, Johnny Haynes. That afternoon he rose to world class.

It had been thought he was anchored to Scottish soil, but Matt changed all that by slipping quietly up to Glasgow, offering the cash on the spot, and persuading the boy that his future lay in Manchester. He cost £56,000 which in February 1963 was a record sum for a wing-half. Looked at now, he was worth double that sum for within three months he had played a major part in their Cup triumph, and then he next helped them carry off the League title in 1965 and 1967.

Nicely proportioned and a first-class reader of the game he has always enjoyed his football with United, and I have always suspected that is partly due to the fact that Law has always proved such an excellent foil and partner. They understood each other perfectly both on and off the park, which one cannot say about many players.

Yet another who always knew what he could and couldn't say to his fellow professionals was Herd, the star whose future was well planned by Dad, while he was struggling with the language. Alec Herd was still a topliner in his own right with Manchester City while David made the daily trek to school in South Manchester. Due to some strange reasoning, the youngster did not become a youthful recruit at Maine Road. Instead, he joined Stockport, then blossomed with Arsenal until Busby bought him for his pack. He was very happy to return north and be among his relatives and close friends once again, was tagged a £35,000 buy which was surprisingly reasonable for 1961, and he added considerable weight to the attack, though not always being everybody's meat.

A considered talker, never willing to rush into anything without examining a topic, he was unfortunately overshadowed by Law during most of his time at Old Trafford, and, additionally, was hard hit by injuries which once threatened to suddenly end his career. He fought back from a broken leg, and then gave Stoke City good service after having scored more than 200 goals in nearly 150 appearances for United.

Herd was always willing to have a go. He took more stick in his seven seasons with the Reds than any other player I have known, yet no one ever saw him dodge a tackle, go over the top, and play unfairly. He was always a credit to the game, and a clean liver. One of the highlights of a great career concerns a game for United against Sunderland, who were then in the First Division. David hit four that breezy afternoon, and the first three were at the expense of different goalkeepers. For when Montgomery went off hurt after being beaten by the first shot, Herd proceeded to beat Hurley, and then Parke. That's one for the book!

TWELVE

The King

MOVING GENTLY through this famous club's history and its equally great personalities we now come to one of the finest of all the fine players they have had, a soccer king in his own right, sometimes a scoring riot, almost always a menace to opposing defences—Denis Law.

From the very first day of his appearance in a red shirt this flaxen-haired, tap dancing, darting and shooting tearaway had the crowd with him. He could send the rabid Stretford Enders into a seventh heaven of delight. Or plunge them into the depths of misery. They applauded and criticised in turn, but none had a good word for him when he first came over the Pennines, because at that time Law was wearing a blue shirt of all colours, and spearheading the attack of their greatest rivals, Manchester City.

The story of this fantastic footballer really needs a full book to itself because he began in such unpromising circumstances, rose to sky-high performances, turned a great industrial city upside down, crossed a Continent, returned majestically, and then refused to be downgraded and made the headlines all over again.

Bill Shankly was his first handler, along with Andy Beattie. So it must be conceded that when he first left his suburban home in Aberdeen as a fifteen-year-old the right coaches were on the job. My old friend Beattie, former Scottish team boss, moved on because just then he felt the pressures of life and the game were becoming too much, and he wanted to refresh himself mentally and physically. Shankly, fully installed as the Huddersfield Town chief, paid particular attention to this slip of a boy who often wore spectacles, stayed home in his comfortable Yorkshire digs every night, and had no yearning for the bright lights or anything like that.

He began developing. He started chasing all the balls all the time in private practice games, and the word got around. Then Shankly played his hand. He slipped the 16-year-old into the Town first team for a Christmas battle with a tough Notts County team, at their own headquarters in Meadow Lane. The Local Press gave it a few lines because, after all, he was a raw teenager making a debut in a line-up that was being gradually remodelled. None recognised that it was a date to be ringed around in red as one of the important occasions in British sporting history. An occasion marking the entry of a new star. But those who defied the elements and saw this gangling, tireless football product with the schoolboy freshness still on his cheeks nip smartly in and out of the home defence were spellbound. So were the odd scouts who had merely popped along because there was no other game in the immediate vicinity. Their messages were going along the grapevine right throughout the following week, and Huddersfield's next match had an unusually large gathering of managers, directors, and their accomplices. All were intrigued about someone so young impressing right at the start, and being backed by no less a shrewd judge than Shankly.

Next, Shankly paired him with Kevin McHale, one year his senior, so that when they faced Burnley it was a wing with a total age of only thirty-three. Some managers admitted to me after it had been announced, that they would not have slept at night planning such an experiment, but Shankly didn't lose any of his shuteye, and the two boys became the talk not only of the town, but of all Britain, with Law claiming most attention.

Everything was going right for the boy. Very soon he became a regular in Scotland's Under-23 team, and on his bow at full level he scored a beauty against Wales, at Ninian Park, with Herd in the No. 9 spot Bobby Collins, of Everton and Leeds, at inside-right. Came the Hampden game with Ireland, and he was home and in his country's shirt before his family and friends for the first time, and it was a controversial affair, as so many of his games have been since.

One of his particular jobs that afternoon of 5th November, 1968 was to blunt the usual effectiveness of Danny Blanchflower, and he certainly limited the effectiveness of the Irish and Spurs right-half with exceptionally close shadowing. Yet it was not until 1960 that the Press accorded him full recognition which I think was largely due to the fact that in those days fewer sportswriters travelled around the country, and in London, at any rate, they rarely knew anything about provincial players unless they happened to be in a top team visiting a top southern club. At that time the old idea prevailed about the map of the British Isles. In the Home Counties they said there was a big blob representing London, and the rest was country.

Well, Huddersfield were drawn against West Ham, in the Third Round, on Saturday, 9th January, 1960, and the venue was their own Leeds Road pitch. They only managed to draw through the odd goal from Law. That suited the Hammers. They staged the replay confidently the following Wednesday, yet once it had started the curtains were always coming down. Because Law was too good for the lot of 'em, completely dominating the tie. He revealed magnificent balance and control on ice better suited to skating, and the Yorkshire club recorded a sensational 5-1 triumph before the staggered hordes of Upton Park. Denis had arrived. The London reporters gave him the best treatment, and wondered how it was they'd missed him for so long. And, of course, the moneyed clubs jealously courted him, assessed their bank accounts, and talked things over with the manager, because everyone knew that if, and when Huddersfield were prepared to part the cash would be a record. Not that there seemed any likelihood of him moving just then, especially with Shankly standing firm and setting his face against any transfer of his rising young star. The manager's line was something about over his dead body. His daily chant was to the effect that clubs which might want him were just wasting their time because they were not going to part at any price.

More than a dozen joined the queue. Shankly refused to change his opinion, and went on saying there was never going to be any parting. But the Huddersfield board had its price.

and that was what really mattered, as it always does. The price gradually rose. Clubs dropped out one by one. Until only Manchester City and Arsenal were left. Some of the morning papers suddenly said it was all over, and wealthy Arsenal were going to take the boy to London within a day or two. I remember drawing the City's manager's attention to these reports because I had been playing them down on private information, and making City club favourites all along. He said : "Forget 'em. He's going to sign for us, and that's that."

And that was that. For Huddersfield eventually fell for the cash bait. Their gates hadn't been good for some time, and the money was big. Big for those days of 1960, anyway. Rumoured at first to be £45,000, and then £50,000, it leaked out it was a little more, and cost folk settled for £53,000. But, actually, it was £55,000—an all-time record fee for British soccer.

Young Denis, bounding about like a ten-year-old after making a lonely journey to Manchester by train, joined a mixed crowd of players at Maine Road. They included internationals from Scotland, Ireland, and Wales, but none from the home country, and though it ended up just an average season for the team the manager wrote in the club's official handbook the next August that he felt justified in predicting a favourable season. It didn't quite turn out that way, even with Law's assistance, and it became the winter of Les McDowall's discontent because rumours suggesting the unexpected departure of young Denis became finalised in the Scot's departure to Italian skies the following summer.

When ten thousand fans went by road and rail to watch Law's debut for City, at Leeds, it had seemed as if he would settle in, and nobody talked any more about the wonderful saves of Bert Trautmann. They licked their lips as they looked forward to his first home game. But he hit only two goals in seven games. Everybody felt, however, that the goals were bound to come, and at a much faster pace the next winter. So they settled back, and waited, expectantly. And the Lawman didn't fail them, though it's got to be admitted they had hoped for more than 19 in 37 League fixtures. Yet he had supplied a touch of colour to the team, excitement to the dressing-room, and liveliness on trips to other towns. Once, when things hadn't gone too well in a home match, he walked around the dressing-room, supplied his own running commentary on everybody's performance, and then analysed himself. He was lonely at first. So, after home games, he often joined one or two other players and myself in a quiet evening drink in "The Parkside", an hotel within a stone's throw of the ground, and there, in a quiet, comfy corner of a deserted lounge we satisfactorily settled all the day's arguments, and, incidentally, often drew up tremendous charters for the good of the game.

He slowly warmed to the comfort of new friendships, and developed into a particularly bright personality, with plenty of time even for the youngest fan. Hannah became his target in the club. He simply could not forget the fact that eleven years before, George and Alf McMichael, an Irish international full-back, had both been transferred from Linfield, the Irish League club, to Newcastle United. Whenever there was a quiet moment the young Scot would turn on Hannah, a quiet, well-balanced type, and open up this way: "How old did you say you are, George? Did you say you're only forty? Well, if that's so, you're not doing badly to be still in First Division soccer."

Hannah, rather surprisingly, always bit the bait. He would turn round on Law, and say: "You jolly well know I'm nowhere near forty." Having roused him, Law used to proceed to "prove" his point by saying: "Well, George, you were eighteen when you started, had eight years with Linfield, another eight with Newcastle, four with Lincoln, and you've already been with City two years."

George used to take a grip on himself, turn round to me, and say: "Don't ever believe what Denis says about me because I'm not forty, and I don't want folk to start thinking I am because I want to stay a lot longer in the game."

He also used to kid Colin Barlow about Lancashire Combination soccer, but never tried taking the mickey out of Leivers. For Bill, a six-footer of bone and muscle who is now managing Cambridge United, always drew himself up to his full height and pushed out his chest and chin as Denis approached in the dressing-room, and then fixed him with his eyes as if to warn of likely penalties for any funny business.

The first time I saw him lose his temper was when City were leading Luton by 6-2, in the Fourth Round of the Cup on the Bedfordshire club's ground in 1961 and the referee abandoned the game just before full time because of torrential rain. He had scored all six in a really tremendous display of power and ball control in atrocious conditions.

When the referee blew them off, they all galloped into the dressing-room soaked to the skin, tossed their shirts and pants away, dragged their boots and socks off, and were in the hot baths before you could say Luton. The City players wondered about the result, and were arguing whether it would stand when I walked in and faced a barrage. I told Law his goals wouldn't count in the record. He looked at me open-mouthed for a moment, then exclaimed : "They must stand because it's no use scoring goals if they don't stand."

He dressed in a black mood, stumped out of the dressing-room, clambered aboard the coach for the airport, and was still very much annoyed when we reached Ringway, and he turned to me with this final comment : "It's an absolute farce that the game was called off after we'd been playing so long, and it'll just be our luck to lose, next week." It was. And the only crumb of comfort they extracted from those night hours was provided by the news which greeted them at Manchester Airport—Manchester United had also lost their Cup replay, going down sensationally 7-2 to Sheffield Wednesday.

Came the summer of 1961, and a club tour of the Austrian Tyrol preceded, unfortunately, by visits from Gigi Peronace, who was then the chief Italian soccer agent. He was determined to get Law for Torino. He recognised he would be a great success over there, and the Turin club were willing to go right to the top in cash bids.

City fought a rearguard action. They didn't want to lose the star it had taken such a struggle to land. So they first of all promised Law extra cash in the hope that he might lose interest in a desire to taste foreign football. But he stayed interested. Eventually, the chairman, Alan Douglas, offered him £100 a week to forget the idea. That was at a time when no other player in Britain was earning anything like such a sum. It was tempting. Yet still Law fancied a trip abroad. The matter was left in abeyance while we undertook the tour, a short one starting with an opening game at Graz, near the Hungarian and Yugoslavian borders, and ending with a final fixture at the Olympic ski centre of Innsbruck, close to the Italian border. We motored leisurely across Austria, through the famous Brenner Pass, wartime meeting spot for Hitler and Mussolini, and it turned out to be Law's last game for City. The only thing that worried him on a country drive the next day, was the need for liquid refreshment in a warm country. He took up the cause of all the other boys by singing a short but effective plea. His high-pitched voice came through the coach—"I want a Coca-Cola; I want a Coca-Cola : I want a Coca-Cola."

Have you ever been cooped up in a Continental bus for mile after mile, and had to listen to tuneless repetition? It was hot, and the miles seemed endless. Someone had to give. It was the manager. He finally instructed the driver to halt at the next estaminet, which he did—rather gladly, I thought. Law dashed off first, and, with a magnificent sweep of an arm, gave one line again, like a victory anthem, and then dashed inside and ordered for everybody at his own expense. When the manager remonstrated, and said the club was paying, Denis replied : " You stopped for me, so I pay the bill." He had faults, like all of us, but was always generous.

Peronace was still hovering around on our return, and eventually got his man. He paid £110,000. City took the money, but were sorry to see the back of the Law-man. Obviously, because it left them with too few good performers for the coming season. From a business point of view it was a good deal. It represented 100 per cent profit on a signing that had been effected only the previous year. One director reminded me of that important factor when we discussed the position, and, though agreeing with the profit motive, I wondered whether it might prove a costly departure.

Admittedly, it meant there would be plenty of extra money in the kitty for buying new stars. But his departure left a bigger gap than most folk had anticipated. City's attack with him in it was always worth a goal or two, but without him it was flat and uninspiring, and, what's more, the new atmosphere in the dressing-room reminded me of flat beer. Gone was the excitement he always created. Everybody missed his breezy personality.

I know they also did at his digs in Withington. That was where they had the task of wakening the boy, and trying to get him away for reporting at the same time as the others. He was nearly always the last to turn up at the ground. Once, in a bid to get him and all the other latecomers toeing the line, a system of fines was introduced on a sliding scale, starting at ten o'clock. It had a salutary effect. Everybody turned up on time—except Denis Law.

He was very happy to get his way, looked forward to Italy, and left Manchester almost as quietly as he had entered it. But he soon missed a big circle of friends. He quickly experienced loneliness once again. I used to write to him, and forward copies of the football edition to keep him in touch with events, and, incidentally, cheer him up for, apparently, life in Turin was very disciplined. At least it was for an expensive soccer import. During most of his time with Torino he shared a flat with Joe Baker, and they said it was the last word in luxury, yet became almost a prison. They went out only very rarely. It was so difficult. If they went to a cinema all was well with the lights low, but once they were turned up and picked out the audience would lose interest in everything else, clamber up for autographs, and talk excitedly in a lingo neither Denis nor Joe understood.

They glanced at newspapers and magazines in shops and on railway bookstalls, but were never purchasers for the simple reason that they didn't know the language. If they slipped into a bar for the odd one there was a riot. Everybody wanted to talk to them. Some others made it their business to inform club officials that they had been seen drinking, and, as usual, reports of that kind always grew with the telling.

At times, the loneliness was hell. That was what Denis

said. So both boys came back. Once it became obvious that Law was becoming unsettled, the Continental switchboard was alerted. He could have picked his club. By that I mean he could have joined any of nearly a dozen. As it was, he returned over his tracks. He landed in Manchester once more. But, instead of taking the Platt Lane bus along Lloyd Street to Maine Road, he caught the Sale bus in Chester Road, and jumped off at Warwick Road, the stop for Old Trafford.

In my time, I've met hundreds of 'em walking into a new club for the first time. Some are brash. Some are a little shy. Others are wondering whether they've done the right thing. Law was a middle course man—a confident young feller, glad to be back among his own Britishers, but not quite so cocky.

It had been a record signing for United. Just as it was when City took him from Huddersfield. But this time it had not merely cost £55,000 to move him to Manchester, but a fantastic £116,000! So, of course, it called for a proper introduction with an eye on maximum publicity, and Matt arranged a Press party in his own little office just above the official entrance to the ground. Sports writers and cameramen from the evenings, mornings, Sundays, and magazines were invited to meet the expensive purchase.

It was almost like a West End first night. We all gathered together in Matt's place, talking and smoking and then suddenly they were there in front of us, the manager and the star. Most of those present had merely seen him play. Few had met him, or really knew him well before he left for the Italian sunshine. He looked lost for a moment. He gazed around for a familiar face and then saw two—those of Arthur Walmsley and myself. Arthur, who was then on the old *Evening Chronicle*, which died shortly afterwards, had also been equally friendly.

Law dashed across the crowded room, shook hands with us, and began chatting away, while Matt waited patiently in the far corner. I whispered that his new boss was waiting to say something, and he stopped talking, turned round to the assembly, and, in a very natural style apologised, and said: "I'm sorry, chaps, but I just wanted a word with these two old friends." Hail-fellow-well-met with nearly everybody, he nearly stood on his head to make certain the photographers got all the pictures they wanted, and answered hundreds of questions, never being the slightest annoyed, even when some of the empty heads tossed foolish ones at him.

There were some football folk who wondered whether United had been wise in paying out that kind of money. After all, it was sufficient to buy up some of the League clubs lock, stock and barrel. Yet Law soon proved the wisdom of that transaction, and had a great first season. He hit 23 goals in 38 League games, and crowned it all with one of the three goals with which they carried off the cup at Leicester City's expense in 1963. It was said with considerable truth that he had very soon paid off a big slice of his fee. The disturbing point was that, without him, things were going from bad to worse just across the way. And when he became The King of the Old Trafford fans, those who followed City set up a mighty groan of despair and annoyance.

Soccer enthusiasts in the Greater Manchester area were perturbed when the Scot suggested he might want a transfer unless his pay packet became a little fatter. And they were upset when it became known the club might do a deal for a cheque around £60,000. Many fancied buying, though held back on doubts about his fitness, especially when he kept staying out of action. In fact, he was struggling to free himself of a damaged hamstring. But he finally silenced everybody by climbing aboard the first-team coach for the short trip to Hillsborough and the F.A. Cup semi-final with Leeds United. He sat out the goalless first-half, and then suddenly re-appeared. It was 14th March, 1970, and he had been the golden boy of the fifties.

It was nothing short of amazing to see the gifted Aberdonian whose dramatic spurts through the penalty box, allied to a magnificent finishing touch had been once applauded by millions trotting out onto the battlefield with an obvious brief for a sharp encounter. There was the Law-man. He moved into the fray. He released his pent-up energies, and suddenly there was danger to Leeds. So far as Denis himself was concerned, it was just what the doctor ordered, though time was running out fast. He got hold of a loose ball, drove for home on the instant, but Gary Sprake flung himself full length to save.

So there was no Law goal to give the perspiring headline writers a break in their constant search for brightness, especially on the early editions, and I felt particularly sorry because at least one sub-editor had cunningly prepared a back page streamer in bold roman caps—King Law Back with the Golden Cup Winner.

I also had sympathy for the player because of knowing how hard he had fought to get back into the big time. Few were aware, yet it was a fact that only three days earlier Denis had turned out in his third match with the reserves. Just a Lancashire Senior Cup tie with Barrow. Nobody could imagine anything less important. But the pitch was heavy, extra time meant the game ran for over an hour and, therefore, provided the right kind of test and, incidentally, taught him that on some other occasions he had returned before being fully fit.

It was an unhappy recall for Law. It was equally disappointing for the sub-editor, who had to be satisfied with this: "United's fight goes on again at Burnden". It reminded me of the time on the *Bradford Telegraph* when Tom Riley wrote one of his rare winners. He was my first sports boss editorially, and when Worcestershire had the nerve to put Yorkshire in after winning the toss at Park Avenue he turned to me and said: "They've got a bloody nerve, Eric".

Well, Yorkshire hit up the runs in next to no time, then bowled out those Worcestershire bounders, and had 'em in and out again before you could even sniff the sauce. Good old Tom, one of the old school, had the sudden inspiration. He flung this splash across the back page of an evening paper which dearly loves its cricket: "Yorkshire relish Worcester sauce". It was a winner, and made his day.

Everybody in sport who moved around in the northern counties, those years, knew Tom, a stoutly-built man with a wonderful moustache. When I first came up alongside him for tuition he used to send me across the centre of the city for a couple of hot meat pies for his lunch. It was a task I didn't appreciate, but I soon found the solution by slipping into an alcove, drinking the gravy, putting them into my pocket, and then walking confidently across town to the office. Once there, I hurried into the toilets, turned on the hot water, and refilled each pie. He never knew, though on one occasion he did call across to dear old Robinson, the chief sub-editor, and say: "These pies aren't as good as they used to be because the gravy's just like bloody water".

Anyway, after a career spanning fifteen seasons, and nearly 500 international, league and cup games Law can look proudly back at the tremendous mark he has made on the game. There are so many wonderful instances of his soccer mastery that it is difficult to nominate the principal. His six-goals-that-didn't-count at Luton came in a really tremendous display, yet again he was fantastic in United's great Cup victory two years later. First of all he cracked an angled shot past Gordon Banks, then saw another drive scrambled off the goal-line after he had left three defenders beaten and helpless, and joined forces with Charlton and Herd in moves that demonstrated soccer at its brilliant best. It's been a privilege knowing him, watching him play, and wishing him many more seasons.

THIRTEEN

Problem Spot

GOALKEEPER. THAT'S not only the No. 1 spot in Manchester United's team, but it has also been the No. 1 problem many, many times. Often it was a position which gave club officials giant-sized headaches between the two wars, and those particular worries have gone on recurring in some amazing way.

Crompton was the ace in the pack when big soccer was resumed in 1946, and if only time had not overtaken him nobody would have worried about picking a man to go between the sticks. But time makes no exceptions, and so dear old Jack, the honoured servant, had to step down eventually, and that signalled the entry of a long procession of successors beginning with Reg Allen, and moving on to Ray Wood, the Hebburn boy who was quietly minding his own business and very happy playing for hard-up Darlington until suddenly hoisted into the top flight with Christmas of 1949 just coming up.

Some of the breaks went against Ray, and it was decided that another 'keeper of experience should be obtained, and the club went out and signed Gregg—on the strength of a brilliant display for the Irish against England's full strength attack at Wembley. On that cold and grey November afternoon of 1957, the six-footer who was taught his soccer ABC in County Derry and graduated with Doncaster Rovers, defied an inside-forward trio formed by Derek Kevan, Tommy Taylor, and Johnny Haynes. The removal fee of £23,500 was a record for a goalkeeper and Harry proceeded to prove his worth with good service, and give little chance to waiting deputies local-boy Dave Gaskell, and Belfast recruit Ronnie Briggs. That is, until the opening month of January 1961. Then, with both

(Left) Bill Foulkes, who came up from the pit at St. Helens to become the regular wearer of the No. 5 shirt

(Right) Alex Stepney, ex-Chelsea and Millwall goalkeeper and voted one of the best in Britain

(Above) Paul Edwards, a young defender from the famous Busby training academy who has got his best years ahead

(Left) David Sadler from Kent hopfields, carefully groomed and now fully settled in

Gregg and Gaskell unfit, the heaven-sent opportunity went the way of young Briggs, the eager beaver who had been learning all the tricks of the goalkeeping trade the hard way.

Having knocked Middlesborough out of the Third Round, United, who had slipped a bit in the race for League honours, were going all out for the Cup, and after earning a Fourth Round replay with Wednesday by sharing two goals at Hillsborough they obviously fancied their chances of winning another brief. But they slipped. Or, rather, Briggs had that kind of game nobody wishes even on their worst enemy. Everything he did went wrong. The Sheffield forwards couldn't believe their luck, yet took full advantage of it, winning by 7-1. It was a fantastic result. On the terraces and in the stands everybody was just staggered. The silence of the morgue descended on the ground as the final whistle died on the wind. Nearly 50,000 pairs of eyes watched Briggs, head down, trudge slowly off the pitch and into the silent dressing-room. One or two players said: "Cheer up, Ronnie". All bathed and dressed as quickly as they could, and left for home. Matt sympathised with the lad. Harry Catterick, the Everton boss who was then managing Wednesday, slipped in to add his sympathies, and later wrote a wonderful letter of encouragement to the distressed young Irishman.

Briggs, to his eternal credit, fought hard to wipe out the memory of that winter's evening, but viewing the unhappy performance in retrospect it is obvious that it ended his possibilities at Old Trafford, and when Gregg packed his bags to take over the managership of Shrewsbury Town, Dave Gaskell took over. The boy from the south Lancashire coalfield around Wigan never became a firm favourite, however, and occasionally Pat Dunne, who learned the business with Shamrock Rovers, had a go while Jimmy Rimmer, the Sandgrounder, was watching from the wings.

Then, suddenly, and without any previous warnings or leakages, Matt caught the morning train to Town, took a taxi from Euston to Stamford Bridge, and signed up a new man for the job—Alex Stepney, a six-footer who must have wondered what the heck was happening to him. Because throughout the previous season he had kept goal for Millwall as they fought for a passport from the Third Division into the Second, and got it. Then this Mitcham youngster was transferred to Chelsea, and before he'd had time to settle in at The Bridge they were saying it had been nice knowing him and pocketing a cheque for £55,000.

You'll remember that United set up a transfer record for goalkeepers when they bought Gregg? Well, they repeated the act with Stepney, who moved north in September, 1966, full of ambition and very soon possessing an England cap, a championship medal and another which was handed to him as a member of the United team which won the European Cup.

So that was a good move? Oh, yes, it was. At the time, at any rate. Later, Alex was not quite so sure because he lost his first team spot to Rimmer, a younger man who had forced himself into the pool and, once nominated as first choice, fought to stay in that category. Originally, Jimmy had climbed onto the bandwagon while Alex was nursing an injury, and didn't worry because of believing he would be restored to the line-up when fit again. But things don't always work out as one anticipates, especially in a branch of sport that's highly commercialised and there is always so much at stake.

Eventually, he asked for a move because reserve team soccer didn't suit him. Just as it never appeals to any star. But the position was carefully and quietly explained to him though, I've no doubt, leaving the player still unsettled. After all, nobody—yes, nobody!—likes stepping out of the glamour, particularly when it means playing in front of empty stands and terraces, and feeling that whatever you do doesn't matter very much. When you're a star in your own right, and you suddenly discover that someone else on the staff is considered the better man for the job it's a blow to personal pride, and also calls for quick re-assessment of the future in case the position doesn't change quickly.

He found it tough, though I reckon that for many others in the same camp the going has been more difficult. Take the case of John Fitzpatrick, the bantamweight from the same Scottish town as Law. He came south to Lancashire eight years ago, but he has not yet completed a hundred first-team appearances although it's recognised that young Fitz is an accomplished performer.

Once he had fought a way through the junior teams and reached official reserve level there was plenty of time for thinking. Came two precious first-team calls during the 1964-65 season, four the next winter, and then another three next time round. Nine big games in three years after a season with the " A " and " B " outfits. Enough to dampen the enthusiasm of most youngsters. But not Fitz.

He went on learning, and improving, and fighting for better recognition until when the records were compiled in the summer of 1968 he was credited with another fourteen matches, which he doubled in the following campaign, and then added another twenty the next time round. There have been occasions when he has been absent because of injuries or suspension, but largely the young Scot has been passed over because others were considered better prospects. When McGuinness was handed the reins he began experimenting, then, finally, decided that it might be better for the player and the club if he was re-styled as a midfield man, where his eagerness to snap into the tackle would not be exposed to the antics of " fall guy " wingers.

Fitz was given an intensive refresher course in the art of making swift and clear cut contact with the opposition, and, if you had asked me for an opinion, I would have said United were remodelling him on the lines of the matured Billy Bremner. Particularly so remembering the way in which he calmly walked away from provocation during the club's summer tour of America twelve months ago.

There were many who were pleasantly surprised to note, on the return from that jaunt to the other side of the world how Fitz, a very sincere soccer disciple, had added maturity to a natural enthusiasm so that the ability came through all the more effectively. Which, I can tell you, was very pleasing to note in a youngster with more than the average share of supporters.

One of his drawbacks has been an unfortunate lack of inches. You may guess that is specially noticeable when he plays against someone like Jack Charlton, and when that point was examined in the pubs and clubs and all the other places where they talk about the game many suggested that Busby should sign some boy like Ron Davies to deal with the high balls. But McGuinness, having heard that one, simply said: "It wouldn't necessarily work out, and for one thing I don't think Davies would move about like Fitzpatrick does."

Stepney and Fitzpatrick are just two who had to fight for ultimate recognition. Like thousands of others in all parts of Europe have to do year in, and year out. And, staying on the same club line, I will now give you another United climber—Tony Dunne, native of Dublin, who went on to lead Eire in the European Nations' Cup, and developed a very loyal habit of saying to all interviewers: "Don't write us off as no-hopers."

I remember talking to this fresh-faced, rather small defender, about his country's chances in that competition, and he seemed to go into a challenging mood almost on the instant. Perhaps that was understandable because as skipper he had been whipping up new enthusiasm among everybody, and said: "We've now got new pride among the lot of us, and every player feels proud and is vitally interested playing for his country which, unfortunately, was not always the case." He was right. For more years than I care to remember, the folk of the Irish Republic had handled arrangements for their national team as if they were planning some village cup game. A committee of amateur selectors used to nominate the team, like it did in the olden days with the English F.A., and players reported to the H.Q. Camp at odd times, some in the evening and others only a few hours before the scheduled kick-off. Now, Tony has helped improve all that, and the team has a professional manager, always gets together at least two or three days before a big game for training and discussions.

Then, again, there is Paul Edwards. It was a struggle staking his claim because there were so many other up-and-coming youngsters nudging him in the long queue for vacancies. Yet when he made the grade everything went right. For a while. Even Sir Alf gave him a pat on the back, and in his first season as an established player he was recruited into the England pool, then called up for the Under 23 game with Bulgaria, in Plymouth, when Derby County's Roy McFarland stood down. Edwards was highly delighted at this kind of progress, as any other youngster would have been. Already, up to that early point, he had figured in many fine games, but I always top the list with the one he played against Leeds, in last year's F.A. Cup semi-final battles of the Uniteds. It was the first of those three clashes to decide Chelsea's Wembley opponents. On that occasion, and before a packed house at Hillsborough, young Edwards outmanoeuvred Don Revie, the master tactician.

It was this way. Edwards, who was having a fierce tussle against a lively and raiding wing, was suddenly injured—twice. First it was the knee, then it was the ankle. The Leeds manager, watching the game closely from the touchline, noted the boy struggle for a brief period, guessed he might be in difficulties against a really fast mover, and smartly switched his players, exchanging the lethal shooting Peter Lorimer for the speed and elusiveness of Eddie Gray.

But the idea hardly ever got off the ground. Not successfully, at any rate. Because this feller from the busy little town of Crompton, perched on one side of the Pennine Range, shrugged off the nagging pain when some might have sought the comfort of the dressing-room and medical attention, and played through his injuries. He completely ignored the pain barrier, became a super defender, and played a major part in holding the champions to a goalless draw.

It was unpleasant journeying home over The Snake. The knee and the ankle were swelling all the time. But he was gloriously happy in the mental playback of the game that had just ended, and disclosed afterwards that when Gray slipped on and Lorimer went off he knew the swap had been effected because Leeds considered he would be struggling against a faster mover—" and recognising that fact kind of kept me on my toes more than ever ". Actually, he was almost robbed of that late performance because McGuinness nearly replaced him. The new boss had worried over the injuries, then noticed the quick Leeds shuffle, and considered substituting Francis Burns until second thoughts introduced a point of caution. That was when Edwards inherited the spot of knee trouble. The plan was cogitated upon again when the boy's ankles came into the line of fire. Fortunately, McGuinness resisted the temptation, and was happy watching his player do him proud.

I would like to have written a wonderful ending to this particular chapter in the full-back's sporting life, but the wind of change spoiled everything. Edwards was moved back into the reserves for a spell, in the winter of 1969-70. The blow fell just after his initial bow in a Young England shirt, and was probably traceable to the fact that the United defence had just previously conceded two easy goals.

Tough? Yes. But in the realms of Big Business Soccer, these days, no error can be contemplated with forgiveness. Somebody's head has to roll each time. Paul probably felt it was a stiff penalty. However, it's an ill wind that blows nobody any good, and the team manager's unexpected decision provided an equally unexpected opportunity for one more teenager—Willie Watson, all the way from Motherwell for a fighting chance with the rest at Old Trafford.

He's just one more to add to that ever-lengthening list of players we've been considering. Indeed, it could be said in all truth a player who seemed to have had it once. That was when the club decided to loan him to Huddersfield Town. He enjoyed getting experience with the Yorkshire outfit, and there's no doubt it improved his general game, but all the time the nineteen-year-old was wondering how he stood at Old Trafford.

Just as he had done at the tail end of the 1969-70 season when suddenly the message came down the grape vine to the dressing-room that United were circularising other clubs with names of youngsters they might be prepared to release. That set him wondering who might be on the list, and whether he was among them, though there's no doubt he felt much better when McGuinness said he would be going on the American tour in the summer.

Of course, the very beginning had brought him right up

against problems. For, after winning Scottish honours at youth and schools' level, he broke a leg while playing for United in a Swiss Youth tourney. But he's got guts, and he fought back not only to fitness but up to the ladder that leads to the spotlight.

On a final nostalgic note of the ups-and-downs of a professional's life we should not sign off this particular part of the club's history without mentioning one I always admired. The name in this case is Seamus Brennan. He gave United fifteen full years of his life until it was decided he was extraneous to their needs. Then they played the game by refusing to make capital out of his departure with a transfer fee and, instead, let him go free, which meant that the full-back could fix his own terms with interested clubs.

If that sounds a little hard, it's not. I've no doubt they could have made some money by listing him with a price against his head, but I've never known them play it that way, especially with good servants. And, on top of that, Shay himself admitted having been well paid and well treated all the time, though, naturally, he felt the break when Matt explained about the parting of the ways. My records show that this fine defender had chalked up 286 League appearances alone since his debut twelve years ago. So it was understandable that the world seemed to have collapsed and the desire for living was evaporating when he reached the end of the road to the club just over the bridge.

He was thirty-two, a proud athlete who had joined them when only sixteen, had travelled the world with the team, and played in scores of great games. Yet if you asked him to nominate the greatest occasion he would say, so simply but with feeling: "The greatest time for me was always just turning up to train with the rest, and know I was a Manchester United footballer."

FOURTEEN

The Astons

IT IS a curious but nevertheless true fact that whenever the talk about big soccer clubs swings over to Manchester United, it is automatically assumed by almost everyone that the Old Trafford outfit have been constant spenders in a sellers market.

I have heard it said hundreds of times that they must have spent three or four million or more in signings. Nothing could be further from the truth. When one remembers their amazing record of continued success over the last three decades it is surprising that they have not paid out huge sums year after year, but figures prove otherwise. They were not concerned in any large scale buying between the two wars, and come to that, few clubs were either. But if we confine ourselves to the last quarter of a century they have parted with only just over £500,000, and looked at in modern light that's almost cheese cake.

Matt plunged only twice in the first ten years of his reign. Then he paid out £29,999 for Tommy Taylor, and £23,500 for Gregg four years later. He added a £45,000 fee for Quixall in 1958, after Jimmy Murphy had spent £26,000 on Ernie Taylor and Crowther. So up to then nobody had been touching the till very much. Admittedly, more cheques have been signed to back up the chase after honours during the last decade, yet even then the total spending for the sixties only just soars past £400,000, and is made up this way—Ian Ure £80,000, Willie Morgan £100,000, Alex Stepney £55,000, Pat Crerand £56,000, Denis Law £116,000. I think that is very firm evidence of careful dealing, especially when one considers that this club is as wealthy as any other in Europe and it would be so easy to pay out without bothering to examine all the pros and cons.

Of course, the boss has never been in favour of building a team out of market purchases. He has always concentrated on a spcial youth policy, and if the Munich tragedy had not happened it's quite on the cards that at least half the sum spent since then would have been saved. But expensive signings have had to be made because some of the youngsters were not ready for First Division soccer, and, unfortunately, have not come through as quickly as anticipated. Some did make the grade, and in that respect I'm now flying a flag for the boy who proved the Stretford End wrong—John Aston, son and heir of the famous Aston family who have talked, breathed and lived Manchester United for nearly two lifetimes. And still say in loud voices that it's the greatest.

Conforming to ritual and opening this particular story at the beginning, we had a nipper named Johnny Aston playing in junior stuff around the Manchester suburbs thirty years ago, with his weather eye always cocked towards the Chester Road, and wondering what was going on there. That was because he had caught the United germ at an age when other boys are just discovering girls. He was an average type winger who was walking on air one evening when he strode over the railway bridge and into the Chester Road after having signed on the dotted line for United. He dreamed dreams every time he turned up for an evening training session, then everything suddenly ended because the Royal Marines decided they wanted a fellow like Aston to help them win the war.

I don't think he did win the war, because I always reckon I did. But he played his part, and when the conflict was over returned in haste to Old Trafford, fearful lest they may not want him if all the rest had turned up first. Luckily, there were vacancies in both the first and second teams, and he concentrated on a wing-half spot until one day when Carey was absent on international duty in Ireland, Matt talked things over with him, then said : " I'm putting you in Carey's place at right-back, and I want to see what you can do, because I've been thinking you'll do best as a full-back."

A hunch? Maybe. But it came off. And he stayed back deep

in the defence becoming the third person of that litany which every boy in Salford, Stretford and the Manchester suburbs knew better than their two times table. It began this way: Crompton-Carey-Aston . . . That's how it always came over the phone from Matt's office, when he was giving out the next match team. Never demonstrative or spectacular, Johnny was a quietly efficient and strong kicking defender who was in the Cup-winning line-up of 1948. when England also handed him the first of seventeen caps. His loyalty was proved when during an England tour of South America in 1950 he was made a tempting offer to board the gravy train and play in Bogota, but turned it down flat. And again he showed what a great clubman he was by suddenly switching positions to help Matt out of a dilemma and making a success in the No. 9 spot.

Fate then stepped in with almost a knock-out blow. He went down ill. It was discovered he had contracted tuberculosis, and the doctor arranged for him to be moved to the North Wales coast, and there in a chest hospital near the holiday resort of Abergele, Johnny spent the next eighteen months, contemplating the joys and sorrows of life, and wondering what else there was in store for him. It was a lonely and quiet life in that hospital overlooking the Irish Sea, and sometimes I wrote him about the passing of time in Manchester.

He recovered his lost health, returned, tried his hand in private business, and then was handed the coaching job after Bert Whalley died at Munich, and he began helping to shape the United stars of the future. One of the boys was his own son, John who was fighting with the rest. That was nothing new for the youngster because he had had a fight on his hands right from school days. Because everybody said he was being favoured by virtue of the fact that his dad used to be an England man.

They always remembered that when he moved through United's reserve teams, and eventually slipped into the League line-up. In fact, it became a disease. So much so that Old Trafford fans used to criticise when there was nothing really to harp on about, if you see what I mean.

When late changes had to be made in the days when he just kept popping in and out of the first team, and it was announced that young Aston was playing the fans who didn't want him groaned to the high Heavens. It was the kind of groan you could hear in the dressing-rooms so it hardly helped the youngster as he faced the testing trial of the run onto the pitch, and the kick-off.

That's not all. They used to shout at him on the field as he quietly went about his job of chasing the long balls and slinging the classy centres across, and managing to score the occasional goal. It wasn't much of a life for the youngster, and many would have handed in their cards, and voted for a quieter living. Or bawled back at the taunting fans. But Johnny did neither. He just bit his lip, never once complained to the boss, and went on playing to the best of his ability.

Largely it was life in the shadow of the brilliance of such ace performers as Best, Charlton, Law, Crerand, Stiles and what-have-you. Even Sir Alf never seemed to sense the developing ability because although he often permutated his boys at under-23 level, he never once sent for this one. Which was an unfortunate error.

Then came *the* day. The day the players were going all out for Matt. Not for themselves, but for the manager. The day they went out to beat Benfica. Everybody had written and talked about United's power being invested in Stiles. Or Charlton. Best or Crerand. But as it turned out the exciting hero of that victory which gave United the European Cup was John Aston junior. He had come into his own when it mattered most with immaculate execution of Benfica's Adolfo. And his game was so great that later the Benfica manager said: "I laid plans for coping with Best, Charlton, and the other stars, but nobody warned me about this boy Aston."

Yes, it was a great date to remember—29th May 1968. When Charlton bagged a pair, Best got one for good measure, and Kidd also moved into the scoring act to the delight of one hundred thousand well wishers who paid £120,000 for the privilege of watching Busby's dream materialise at last.

It had been no easy jaunt. Take that from a keen and critical examiner of the drama which stretched over eight exciting months from one Autumn to the next Summer, and began with a visit from Hibernian, the everlasting pride of Malta. The men from the George Cross Island were followed by Sarajevo, Gornik and Real Madrid until we reached the famous twin towers and the day of destiny.

It was anticipated that United might just have the pull forward, and certainly had the half-back strength with such a line as Crerand-Foulkes-Stiles. But the possibility of the killer punch coming from outside-left was not canvassed very much. Yet that is exactly what happened because young John, who by then had only three full seasons of first-team soccer experience behind him, was the man of the match.

The fans, like everybody else, have poor memories of the stars, and even the biggest names soon fade, and they begin saying : " I seem to remember that fellow. . . ." They treated John better when the next season opened, but his luck didn't stay with him and he made a meagre thirteen League appearances that following winter, and only twenty-one the next, though, altogether, he is now heading towards his two-hundredth appearance for the club which is pretty good for a boy who got such a raw deal from the fans in the early days.

FIFTEEN

Nobby

MANCHESTER UNITED have been short of cash on many occasions in their turbulent history, but they have never lacked personalities of one kind or another, and can now claim to have possessed at least one of the greatest characters this old game of ours has ever known—Nobby Stiles. A little fellow who was reared and educated and taught to stand on his own two feet in an overcrowded northern suburb of Manchester, he is a man who split the world in two until one half loved him, and the other half hated him.

A family man who is glad of home life and all its attendant responsibilities, he has an extremely large circle of good friends who appreciate his cheerful though quiet manner, sincere outlook, and an obstinate resolve against ever being connected with anything underhand or dubious, and is forever careful in everything.

That is Stiles off the park. On it, he becomes an entirely different individual person as if a Guru had mysteriously injected fresh, red blood into his veins, and then poured fire over all his sixty-six inches. To such degree that many claim he is the most hated of all international footballers, a distinction shared with nobody.

Otto Gloria, the well known European coach, sniffs the air when you mention the name Stiles, and always calls him an " unfair player ". The South Americans refer to him briefly and pungently as " The Assassin ". When Sir Alf Ramsey surprisingly included him in England's World Cup Squad as plans were being shaped for last year's battles in Mexico most folk said it was a message to the Brazilians that the England team boss was not going to be intimidated. Backing up that view, Don Revie opined that it indicated we were not going to be pressurised into scrapping the tenacious style of play which swept us to success in 1966.

There were thirty names on that early list, yet everybody at once concentrated on the inclusion of Nobby, who over the last few years has been the victim of a remarkable hate campaign in almost every match he has played outside these shores. It's a vendetta which has always annoyed those who know him well, but I suppose it is one which has gone on thriving because he always looks so damned fearsome on the field, and even Busby, who considers the criticism unfair once said to me, when we were talking about Stiles : " He has never hurt anyone, but I'll admit he's frightened quite a few."

Coming nearer home it is difficult to categorise all the opinions of the stands and terraces on British grounds, but I must say he is cheered and loved in his home country when wearing the white shirt of England. That was adequately underlined by the tremendous whoop of joy which rose over our green and pleasant land when Sir Alf pencilled in his name.

It's a different matter, however, when he steps down to club level and pulls the bright red shirt of Manchester United over his head. Then backers of other clubs begin to loathe the very sight of him. For full evidence of this you only had to slip up to Maine Road for a " Derby " game. There was absolute silence as the early members of Matt's team came trotting down the tunnel and onto the pitch—because every Manchester City supporter was waiting for Stiles. And when he appeared a tremendous hiss spread around that great bowl just as if it was some Victorian melodrama and little Nobby was a moustache-twirling knight interested only in the virginity of the City maidens.

One can never forget the reception accorded him on returning to the game after a long lay-off with cartilage trouble. He had begun to lose faith in himself and his ability to hit the top when suddenly England said they might want him again on the other side of the world. Then he was reminded that, in any event, United had need of him. So he motored from a club lunch to Maine Road with the rest. Once more there was the mighty hiss accompanied by boos and whistles as the homely product of Collyhurst stepped onto the stage. Yet I happen to know that as the chorus was taken towards him on the wind it was like a magnificent symphony. It was even better music to his ears when now and again some irate City supporter yelled out : " You dirty little bugger ".

Again, he was ploughing into the kind of bone-crunching tackles that have made them wince all the way from Manchester to Milan, and hundreds of other far-off places, too, and when he won the ball and walked away there was that identical expression of joy which millions in all parts of the world saw on their TV screens when England became champions at Wembley—a look of nothing else but sheer, unadulterated and toothless bliss!

He has had it tough for donkeys' years, yet never pleaded for sympathy. It seems as if that kind of crowd treatment acts like the sustenance of a bottle of how's-your-father or an old vintage wine from the Rheims champagne cellars on a tired traveller. Obviously, he likes it that way, and, in fact, once said that when they stop booing he'll start worrying because it would mean he wasn't doing his job.

Which rather brings me to another and very interesting facet of his game, and it's just this : the players don't kick up Old Harry about him. And I can't remember a single professional complaint, whereas, on the other hand, he has often been the recipient of complimentary remarks. Once, Malcolm Allison, the Manchester City coach, paid him this tribute : " It is good to have a man on your side who is so totally committed to winning." Goalkeeper Gordon Banks, who must have often been glad to see his back, says : " When Nobby's around everyone has got to do their job ", and Jack Charlton adds : " He's the sort of player you'd want in any side."

Johnny Giles, Leeds United's Eire international inside-forward, and Nobby's brother-in-law, believes that he has been more responsible for the success of Bobby Charlton at club and international level than any other single person in the game, his reasoning being that as Charlton is not a particularly good tackler he relied heavily on Stiles winning the ball for him in midfield, just as Roy Paul and Dave Ewing often used to win it for Revie.

If you meet this little soccer warrior who is so meek and mild off duty he will talk to you about Old Trafford, admit to being a United fanatic from his schooldays, and then add that his confidence always improves tremendously once he gets the sniff of an England shirt.

On that score, Nobby says : " I'm a nationalistic man, and my country means a lot to me, so you can imagine how proud I've always felt whenever I've played for England, because it means I'm out there fighting for millions." On the score of dedication at all levels, he says, very honestly and simply : " Ever since a boy I've hated the attitude about having to be good losers, which seemed to be prevalent in English teams in all international sport at one time, and when I play I play to win though I don't know about this reputation for toughness because I've never been in a fight in all my life, and if one started I'd be getting out of it as soon as I could."

That's Nobby. The real Nobby, who has been worrying about the future either as a defensive wing-half or something else. He has faced the same problem that thousands before have had to do when they've been nearing the thirties and younger men have been quietly moving into the spot they had thought were theirs for keeps.

The problem first arose when injury pulled him out of the team, and those in charge had to experiment in a brave bid to discover a stand-in who might be the permanent answer or, at least, the readymade successor for any other occasions which might arise. David Sadler, the young six-footer and a Kentishman to boot, who had been plucked from junior grade in the Home Counties, was given Nobby's job, and caught Sir Alf's wandering eye. He became one of the best occupants of the No. 6 spot in Britain, eventually winning an England cap, and, of course, setting both Busby and McGuinness a king-size problem. It's nice to have an embarrassment of riches, though it usually carries with it the necessity for diplomatic handling of tricky positions. Like the one which was created when Sadler filled the bill and Stiles stayed in the queue.

(Right) Francis Burns, a fullback who is fast off the mark and going right to the top

(Below) John Fitzpatrick —Fitz to all the Stretford Enders—is another youngster who has come on a ton and is a continuing credit to the old Aberdeen town of Law

(Above left) John Rimmer is the goalkeeper who is always staking his claim to the No. 1 spot and never stops fighting for it

(Above right) Tony Dunne, like his colleague Burns, lacks a bit of height, but that's all that this Irish fullback is short of

(Left) Frank O'Farr appointed in June 19 to take over from Matt as manager

They found him another job as an inside-right. Then he became an inside-left, a right full-back, an outside-right, and so on. But never a left-half until one day Sadler was a casualty, and Nobby slipped back into his old glory spot, and, what's more, played with all the old flair and fury. It was an intriguing situation which was later resolved by Sadler taking over once again, as Stiles, after ruefully checking the team sheet merely said : " The boss picks the team, all I can do is play my best in the reserves."

He did. He even gave everything in a game with Cheshire Leaguers Ellesmere Port, on Merseyside. But it was sad to see him in the anonymity of soccer at that level, an ace of whom Arsenal's Bob McNab once said : " If you make a bad pass he'll shout at you, and swear at himself when he does the same ". And Sadler added : " When you're playing for Manchester United he tells you off for making a bad pass in a practice match."

Now he's moved up to Middlesborough, and everyone is hoping that the transfer works out well, as it could do because he is nowhere near the end of the road.

When he does eventually call it a day we shall forever remember how his socks always rolled down and he walked around in a world of his own, while those who hated his ability and his guts always criticised. For me the best memory spotlights Bolton, and the F.A. Cup semi-final replay with Leeds. The referee awarded a free kick to Revie's boys. It annoyed Stiles. He leapt fully three feet into the air with rage, and, on coming back to earth, slipped and measured his length on the Burnden pitch. Everybody in that crowd of 50,000, and all the players and match officials roared with laughter. Stiles looked up. He gave them the famous glare, and then smiled himself. Stiles the Assassin? Never!

SIXTEEN

Rainbow's End

EIGHTY-THREE mixed years of adversity and success had gone by when at long last Manchester United came to the end of the rainbow, the moment in life Matt Busby had planned and pined for ever since it became a possibility—the final battle for a prize which carried with it the title of Champion Club of European Champion Clubs—The European Cup.

It was the trophy which the F.A. and the League tried snubbing in the early days, because of being jealously aware that it might become a bigger crowd puller than any of their own domestic fixtures. It was also the magnetic prize for every ambitious British club almost from the very start. Most of all United. For both their chairman and manager had it in their sights when clubs were first canvassed, and, defying authority, entered the competition in its second year.

It was in the winters of 1956 and 1957, when they first made their presence felt by demolishing Anderlecht, going through to the second round with the startling winning aggregate of 12-0. Borussia Dortmund were next to crumble before their strength, followed by Atletico Bilbao. But Real Madrid punctured their semi-final hopes, though, in so doing, the triumphant Spaniards, top Continental team of that era, gave Busby the extra appetite and desire to be the first English club to beat off the entire challenge of Europe.

They had another go the following year, but had to admit defeat again in the semi-final, and met with a similar fate in 1966. So it was becoming a kind of a bad habit. One to get rid of, as Matt knew very well. And that was the kind of mood he was encouraging when, after they had stormed their way to the League championship of 1967, they braced themselves for the bigger thing, and disposed of Malta Hibernian, Sarajevo, Gornik Zabrze, and then Real Madrid in fairly quick succession. It was Wembley's turn for the final, and the billing of a match between United and Benfica, the Portuguese champions, who had already carried off the prize, promised a full house and a great game. It didn't quite turn out that way because no one could say the football could be classed as Wembley's best but the result was highly satisfactory, and must have delighted millions not only in the United Kingdom but in scattered parts of Europe and farther overseas. For the club's name has spread to the four corners of the earth, made even better known through the Munich disaster. Naturally, almost everybody who lived within a reasonable distance of Old Trafford was geared for the fray, and there was such a vivid splash of red spreading around the stadium when the teams came out that it struck me that United had worked a cunning flanker. They had turned it into a home match!

It was one of those bone crunching starts which made it clearly apparent to all that the Portuguese were determined to either quieten Best or put him out of the game. For he was floored heavily no less than five times in the opening quarter of an hour. It was amazing how the Irishman controlled his temper, and equally fantastic why Cruz was never even booked. But he wasn't, and it looked likely to further develop into an assault on George until that man Stiles came into the scene, looked around at the Benfica villains, employed one of his hefty charges on Eusebio, and the position quietened a bit.

There were no goals in a first-half rather of meditation and probing than assault and finishing, but it did appear as if United were on a winner with a fine scoring header from Charlton, on the fifty-third minute, but Graca nullified it with an equaliser seven minutes from the end of normal time. So they rested in groups on the pitch, and that was when Matt once again proved his extra ability. For he bent down to speak to first one and then another, and gave a quick talk to one bunch, all the time encouraging, guiding, supplying the kiss of life.

The odds were even when they returned to the battlefield like giants refreshed, and I was particularly glad to see Best take the mickey out of Benfica in the best possible way by moving onto a pass from Kidd, jinking through as only he can, and, after challenging the goalkeeper to come out, pushing the ball round him and rolling it into an empty net. To the staggered astonishment of every Portuguese player. But to the frantic delight of his own team mates, and every supporter of United's cause.

It was a goal to set before a King. And it marked the beginning of a seven-minute span in which the boys from Old Trafford completely destroyed the opposition. For after Best had chalked up his effort on the ninety-third minute, Kidd celebrated his nineteenth birthday with a scoring header two minutes later, and Charlton made it 4-1 on the hundredth minute. They were home and dry while playing out the rest of extra time.

Now to the finish, and the heartwarming scene of delight. In all the years of attending the Wembley annual feasts I never witnessed quite such a scene. Matt bobbed in and out with commiserations for his opponents then let his hair down in a glorious moment with his own boys, who were besieged by others before going into the lap of honour. A lap not merely to celebrate the fact that they had at last won *the* trophy, *the* prize, but to gleefully and with great spirit underline the more important point that they had annexed the senior award of the Union des Associations Européennes de Football for The Boss—Matt Busby.

For the record, United generally appeared better equipped both in defence and attack on that historic evening of Wednesday, 29th May, 1968, even though the great Denis Law was absent while recovering from the effects of an operation. Perhaps neither Charlton nor Best was sufficiently prominent, but it was most satisfying to note the creditable performances of such youngsters as Kidd and Aston, who were at that time really moving through the era of development.

Foulkes earned stars for the way he played Torres, and there must be special mention for Stepney who, after looking slightly uncertain in the early stages, played tremendously well, and had the considerable satisfaction of finally being commended by the very man he thwarted on several occasions —Eusebio.

Best lived up to his name as a marksman, hitting four in the nine games of the competition, while Sadler was next with three, Charlton and Law each had two, and Foulkes, Aston and Kidd one apiece. Further details show that they also proved the most attractive of all the competing clubs pulling in 628,000 spectators with a team which only cost £224,000 to assemble because just four had had to be bought—Law (£116,000), Stepney (£52,000), Crerand (£52,000), and Dunne (£5,000). Nothing was spent on the rest of the pool—Burns, Foulkes, Sadler, Stiles, Best, Charlton, Kidd, Brennan and Aston. Which must have been additionally satisfying to Busby, a man always so keen on home-made stuff.

He returned home thinking of some even higher peak to climb, and, of course, that was the world club championship, which meant them tilting with none other than the big shots of the South American game—Estudiantes de la Plata, who used to be one of the Chico clubs of the Argentine, and went right to the top when they knocked out the South American champions and World Club Cupholders, Racing Buenos Aires.

Great believers in youth, their line-up usually has an average age of only twenty-two, most of whom possess University degrees, which accounts for the fact that their stars are either fully qualified doctors, lawyers or dentists who leave the game for private practices at the end of individual contracts.

Immediately they were contacted, everything was action. Officials flew over unannounced for a secret look-see, checked back on everything likely to be of value in their match planning, and then went back to their own playground and briefed the boys day after day until United arrived. The temperature gradually rose, and, as it turned out, the game itself matched the scorching heat and set up the fiercest of controversies almost across the face of the earth.

Actually, the taste of things to come was supplied by Estudiante officials just before the vital date. They contacted

Matt at his hotel and suggested that it might help lower pre-match tension, and, in turn benefit the match itself, if a friendly little party was arranged at some pleasant, quiet rendezvous some distance outside the city which, just then, was packed with excited soccer fans, most rooting for the home club, and letting everybody know it, too. It looked a jolly good idea, and it was agreed that United would drive out the twenty-five miles shortly after lunch. But when they reached the place there was no sign of anybody connected with Estudiantes. Eventually an official turned up to say there had been some kind of misunderstanding and their boys were resting elsewhere. Or something like that. Anyway, it had all the trade marks of a fast one. Matt was very angry at having made a wasted trip, and then having to drive another twenty-five miles back to their H.Q.

It was nothing less than a brawling, bad tempered first leg in La Plata, during which Stiles got marching orders, and the home boys ended one goal up before the final whistle. It all meant that everybody on this side of the world realised that the Argentinians were determined to keep their title at all costs and that the return game would be one nobody should miss.

So, on Thursday, 16th October, 1968, exactly three weeks after the first battle, they met again for bloody slaughter, and on that occasion Best was sent off, and, as each side scored once Estudiantes were champions by virtue of that solitary one they had obtained on their own pitch.

It was an unsatisfactory pairing in almost every way, though looked at from a financial point of view it meant that United benefited to the extent of about £25,000. But that was the only reward after a host of lost tempers, a bit of sharp practice, annoying refereeing, body bruising in wholesale fashion, two stars having to pay the extreme penalty, and twice crossing the Atlantic. Yet I've no doubt at all that Busby will have another go at that world title just as soon as his boys once again become English champs, and then European champs.

It's going to be difficult winning all three. The first is always a distinct possibility for a club of United's reputation, expertise, and wealth, and the second can be accomplished as Matt has proved to our complete satisfaction. But when you're up apart against these folk who live and play according to different rules in another Continent the problem immediately assumes new and different difficulties.

What really mattered most to Manchester, Lancashire, and, yes, English people just then, I think, was that it had been a great year for a club which had been great, then stricken down, and risen from the ashes to world class again. It had also been Matt's year. That was it. Matt's year. And rightly so when you remember that he was voted into the most honourable position of Manager Of The Year.

SEVENTEEN

The Very Best

WHEN SIR MATT BUSBY was leaving Buckingham Palace after being knighted shortly after the European Cup triumph, a young girl standing near the Queen Victoria monument ran towards the car, and called out in a strident voice: "Have you brought George Best with you?"

I don't think the Manchester United chief saw or heard the youngster, but the incident, nevertheless, proved yet once more what an amazing hold this Irish boy exercises over the teenagers in all parts of Britain.

I have never known anything quite like it. That's a fact. In forty years of watching and writing about the stars, and mixing with the Top Brass, I cannot recall any player who has gripped the fans' imagination quite so much. And in making that point I am remembering such former crowd pullers as Hughie Gallacher, Dixie Dean, Stan Matthews, John Charles, Peter Doherty, and Alex James. They had tremendous followings, but nothing to compare with this recruit from the Belfast suburbs.

Who is this fellow? What's he done to earn such remarkable appraisement? He was one of many hundreds who learned the elementary rules of the game in schoolboy soccer around the Northern Ireland capital until old Bob Bishop happened on the scene, noted the promise, and made a mental note to have another look. Bob, who has now been scouting the six counties on behalf of United for over twenty years, watched him again, and was finally impressed by a shrimp of a boy who badly wanted to try his luck in England. That was way back in 1962, almost about the same time that everybody was talking about the world record transfer—the signing of Law by Manchester United, at a cost of £116,000.

Law was the name. The BIG name. Nobody else mattered in top soccer, either on the park or on the stands and terraces. Best got his first glimpse of the Law-man from the touchlines, along with the rest of a bunch of hopefuls who were pulling out all the stops in every practice and reserve game. Eventually, after filling out a wee bit, he caught the eye of Murphy, and then Busby. And on Saturday, 14th September 1963, played First Division soccer, operating on the right-wing for United against West Bromwich Albion.

Since then he's been on the escalator, going up most of the time, coming up against authority now and then, winning more Irish caps every year, and fascinating millions with his football. Undoubtedly a genius. A permanent five-starred enemy to all opposing defences. A landowner in the stockbroker belt of the pleasant County of Cheshire with an annual income in the £25,000 bracket.

The old prophet said that each man in his time plays many parts. That is particularly true of Best. For, after playing the juvenile lead in schools' soccer across St. George's Channel, he is now filling the widely contrasting parts of footballer, businessman, boutique owner, sports writer, model and heartbeat.

Sometimes one finds him posing under the glare of studio lights with a lovely blonde adoringly on his shoulder for a fashion picture which will sell thousands of whatever they publicise. On other occasions, he is busily selling his name as a brand for something or other; and on top of everything is now under contract to United for a further eight years which guarantees him another £100,000.

Nice work if you can get it. And very pleasing, too, for the fellow on the receiving end. But an overall assessment of the position also requires knowledge of other angles, and so his value to the game should be underlined. For it is a fact that he is still the biggest drawing card in European soccer today. Any chairman of a top club will quickly tell you that when it's known Best is going to be in a visiting United team, thousands more roll up. There was the instance of last year's five-a-side soccer tournament at Wembley. Tickets were selling rather slowly. Once it was announced that Best would be in United's fivesome they went like wildfire, and thousands kept hanging around for the odd chance of being able to pick up the odd stray one.

It might be said that his tremendous personality pulled them in. Maybe it was because folk wanted to watch his dancing feet. Or his impishly sad smile. What they did see was sure proof of his extraordinary ability for exhibition football. One cannot quickly forget, if ever, the amazing way in which he suddenly faced a line of Crystal Palace tackles and destroyed them one by one with magnificent control. And how he miraculously adjusted the pace of the game against a very efficient Spurs challenge.

He forgets everything else and becomes engrossed in the game when he's playing, but it's difficult to forget his own image once he's left a sports arena. Even when he is having one of his occasional nights out fans and spongers clutter up the place. He used to enjoy quiet evenings in the digs before moving into the new home. A meal of braised steak, fruit salad topped with ice cream, and biscuits was very satisfying, as was the half pound of milk chocolates he ate through while sitting in front of " The Box ". Sometimes now he looks terribly bored when out with friends in their favourite trendy bars. Mostly the talk is about films, of which he is a great fan, particularly of westerns, and thrillers, and especially the one titled : *A Man Called Horse*. If there's nothing much new on the silver screen, they venture forth on a quiz, leading to the chin for the nearly knockout with this one : Name the men who formed the cast of *The Magnificent Seven?* Everybody stumbles over it while they roar with laughter at the ignorance of people.

You may be wondering who the seven were, and hating me for raising the point and keeping you awake all night. Most of those questioned, however jump in quickly with the names of James Coburn, Steve McQueen, Charles Bronson, and Yul Brynner. Then they hesitate. Someone remembers Horst Buchholtz. Then Robert Vaughn. Rarely does anyone identify the seventh—Brad Dexter. Harmless stuff, of course, as they float from one discotheque to another with over-amplified records assaulting the earm drums, and rooms of various shapes, sizes and decorations are packed or nearly empty according to their popularity.

Essentially shy, he clings to old and trusted friends, tries to dodge the inevitable scroungers and heartbreak retailers, and pays no attention to abusive writers and telephone callers, though he was a bit annoyed when one fellow began threatening to blow up his new house, and wondered whether the chap really didn't like him, or if it was just a case of someone with a mania for destroying property.

There have been occasional clashes with the law over his beloved cars, but he believes it all depends on the type one is driving. During the period when he had a yellow Lotus Europa the police were always stopping him for one thing or another. When he swapped to a Capri, and then an Executive Zodiac nobody bothered him at all. But he anticipated all that quiet would end when he went back to an E type.

Busby, Murphy, McGuinness and the rest of those loyal to United, and, of course, all soccer fans hope that whatever car he adopts in the future his soccer game won't change, and then maybe he will be able to break all previous club appearance records. For, though it's not been noted by many, the Irishman is nearing the position from which he could contemplate such a feat. According to my records, he is already nearing 300 League games, and if every first team fixture is added George is moving nicely towards the 400 mark. That is an exceptionally fine performance for a player of only twenty-four, who has contracted to keep on playing for the Old Trafford club until he is thirty-one. By then he'll perhaps be feeling a little old. At least, much older than just now. But I should warn him that no man is really old until his mother stops worrying about him.

At any rate, I'm not looking forward to the days when Old Father Time taps him lightly on that right shoulder, because British soccer will be losing not only an artiste but also a character to whom Don Revie, one of the great managers of this present era, once paid the highest possible tribute by saying that " the best chance any team has of beating Manchester United is to shackle Best and Charlton because they are world class forwards who can win matches on their own."

I like to hear praise of that kind from hardened professionals because it helps the cause of youngsters like Christopher Masters, probably Best's smallest fan. He's only three year of age but thinks so much of George that he refuses to answer to his own name—but responds like lightning if you call out : " Georgie Best, are you there?"

I also remember with warmth the twin months of January and February, 1969. Best was suspended for a month following an alleged incident after the League Cup semi-final, and, therefore, spent a period of enforced idleness while the team was fighting its way through the first tough period of the year. He returned to action on Saturday, 7th February, and United welcomed him back because that particular afternoon they had a Fifth Round Cup engagement on the " pocket " ground of Northampton Town, where the crowd gathers on three sides, and the fourth is almost open to the county cricket pitch.

Everybody in that busy centre of the huntin' and shootin' country was taking time off to queue for places because the great Manchester United team had come south with George Best in the attack. Every Dad was taking his boy along to see United, but with special instructions to note Best, and that's how they were talking as the club coach moved slowly up alongside the official entrance, and the *Great Ones* stepped out.

They pointed out the stars one by one. Then, as a lithesome half-smiling figure appeared on the exit steps of the coach, you could hear a murmur. Everybody was saying to everybody else : " That's George Best ". Just as if it was The Man From The Moon. They gaped. Some reached out to touch his sleeve, and be able to tell the thrilling story to their friends the following week.

Well, the game began between the First Division team and the home club which had enjoyed one brief season in the top circle and then descended to the Fourth Division again. There were just a few preliminary skirmishes before Busby's boys took charge, and won rather pleasantly by 8-2, and no fewer than *six* had been obtained by the boy with the touch of the blarney stone. It was a scoring semiquaver that won sports headlines in every corner of the earth.

He was pleased. Very pleased. Especially as he had had quite a lot of misgivings about the game, for, as he said: "The team had been playing very well without me, and I was wondering whether I might be blamed if anything had gone wrong and we'd lost or struggled for a draw, especially as some writers had suggested that the team would be better off without me in it." You'll agree that was hardly a good attitude of mind in which to approach a game meaning so much to his fellow professionals and the club. But, as usual, once the game had started he forgot that worry. He gave a first-class performance.

Yet there was no air of boastfulness on coming out of the dressing-room. First of all, this socialite with the growing look of the Icelandic explorer, who affects gold rings on the second and third fingers of the right hand, where they are joined together by a thin, gold chain, said to the bunched crowd in the tiny corridor under the main stand: "The goals just kind of happened, and honestly I didn't consciously go out to score a lot, and I'm certain the rest of the boys weren't just playing to me, but that's how it happened."

In between expressing some surprise, rather apologetically as if he didn't want any blame for that sixsome, he kept turning round to sign the autographs of the Northampton players, then made for the exit, and the coach which by then was ready to depart. Some of the other boys banged on the windows. They were getting restive, and wanted to be off. So he moved smartly to the open door at the end of the corridor. A white-faced young boy cosily wrapped in an invalid wheel chair looked up from his well-thumbed little autograph book. He had been specially allowed to stay there for a while after the match so that he might collect some new names. Matt Busby had already signed. So had many others. But here was The Big Star. The boy sat quite still. He didn't think he'd be lucky. But he was. George saw him, dropped his own case, fumbled for a pen, took the book, and signed it. Then he had a few words with the youngster, whose delight was shining from his eyes. Best had won a new fan for the rest of his life.

That's his warm side, and it's only right that it is instanced, because so much is written about the other side. Like the story in a London paper to the effect that he was going to give up money and girls to make himself a better footballer. Just imagine it. A healthy, bright young fellow of twenty-four thinking of cutting adrift from everything. Just as if he was going to live in a monastery. Maybe it is difficult reconciling a full-time athlete's life with some of the available pleasures, but at the moment, at any rate, a little bit of burning the candle a both ends is certainly not having any great effect on his footballing ability. Especially on the amazing way in which he recovers after being tripped, and goes jinking on his way.

That was a point which struck me when in one game, last season, he was tripped deliberately at least six times. He never came a purler flat on his face, but, instead, somehow maintained his balance and went forward, whereas ninety-nine per cent of other players would have ended up measuring their length, and been awarded a free kick which often, would be to the advantage of Best. But that's one advantage he is not awarded because of his better balance and ability—this man whom some would turn into a teetotaller, woman hater and anti-socialite in order to remain a good player.

What does Busby say about him? Quite a lot, of course. Sometimes it's in defensive mood, on other occasions praising the boy who grew up into the kind of man who puzzles Matt, who says just this : " There is nothing I like better than to see George's black thatch bobbing about among the young players during a practice, because he enjoys and loves the game so much until he's as daft about football as the daftest of the fans."

That was how he played against Chelsea, in the League Cup, last season. He loved the game. And the manner of it also suited someone perched comfortably in the main stand. It was a small, quiet man who had especially crossed the herring pond to watch this particular match.

A huge smile fluttered across his face every time the Best

boy took over. He was entitled to smile. Because Bob Bishop was looking at the finished product of the youngster he sorted out from the rest in Belfast junior soccer these nine years ago.

EIGHTEEN

Bobby's Patch

BIG JACK CHARLTON always says on looking back over his career that one thing which influenced him very much in becoming a soccer professional was a " bloody great hole in the ground at Ashington ". He meant the local pit down which most of the men in the Northumbrian colliery town worked, and where it looked as if he might join his Dad if he didn't get fixed up elsewhere.

That could have been the same prospect for brother Bobby, though he was beginning to take an interest in engineering nearing the end of schooldays because Mother insisted that he must safeguard his future, with a tradesman's card to provide the permanent passport to jobs.

Murphy completely changed that outlook after both Dad and the boy had been transported south, taken around the Old Trafford set-up, and told of the prospects and all the rest. That was in the autumn of 1954, when he was only rising to seventeen. Now today, he's a family man who makes a daily 28-mile round trip in his red Rover saloon, linking United's Stretford headquarters with his detached home in the tree-lined avenue haven of Lymm, the beautiful Cheshire village retreat for wealthy Manchester businessmen and all others who can afford to live in the place.

There's no doubt about it, he's certainly got a season on the gravy train. He knows it. For he admits that almost every morning as he is driving towards Old Trafford, he appreciates what football has done for him and his family, and, because of that honest realisation, feels a strong sense of responsibility to all who support the game, especially the fans who brave the winter storms on the terraces.

Bobby puts it this way: "Thousands of people pay out their hard-earned money to watch us play, and the least we can do for them is to try all the way so they'll go home feeling that it's all been worth it." I would say that the big majority who have watched this unassuming star play his heart out week after week, and year after year will be ready to say he has given them full entertainment and enjoyment, and not let anybody down.

I can vouch for the fact that he has not changed one little bit except in losing most of the pleasant thatch he had when first making the United League team. He was just as shy in those far-off days, hardly saying a word to anyone when flying out to Ireland for one of his early caps, and only becoming a little talkative when the night plane was nearing Manchester, and he turned to me excitedly, and said: "You see that black patch down there, well that's Old Trafford just alongside Chester Road."

That black patch remains for all observant people to note as the night pilots put the nose down for cruising into Ringway, but the place on the Park side of the permanent way has undergone tremendous change, developed into a world name, and, at the same time, helped to boost the Charlton stock.

Today, Robert Charlton, skipper-extraordinary of the Manchester United Football Club, and holder of the Esteemed Order of the British Empire, knows he has come a long way since first seeing the light of day in a terraced home in the colliery township of Ashington on 11th October, 1937, picking up the vowels at Hirst North School and Bedlington Grammar School in between playing for the East Northumberland schoolboys, and then for England in five school internationals.

Quite a mouthful? Yes, and so is the description of the full cap trail from a Hampden debut on 19th April, 1958, and subsequent matches against practically every soccer-loving country. To wit: Portugal, Yugoslavia, Russia, Italy, Brazil, Peru, Mexico, U.S.A., Sweden, Spain, Hungary, Luxembourg, Austria, Argentina, Bulgaria, France Czechoslovakia East Germany, Switzerland, Uruguay, Eire, West Germany,

Rumania, Holland, Finland, Netherlands, Norway, Poland, and, of course, Scotland, Ireland and Wales.

No wonder the Football Association presented him with a silver salver when he had made one hundred appearances in the white shirt and the distinguishing badge of the lions rampant. And it was also a very good thought to attach the countries' flags to the salver though I could never understand why Holland's colours were missing.

The international slant on the balding Bobby is perhaps best provided by Sir Alf Ramsey, who inclines to the view that although the United man has become a good reader of the game, he was often totally inspired by a simple desire to get at the ball without examining the prospects.

On that particular theme, the England team boss says: "In my opinion, he was a good player, and then a very good player for some time, but did not become a great one until suddenly during our match against Yugoslavia in May of 1966. It was our last game at Wembley before the World Cup. He was in mid-field when our attack broke down on the left-wing, and he would have normally and instinctively chased the ball out to that wing. But he didn't. He suddenly halted, just as if remembering something, and looked all around him. When the Yugoslav defence switched the ball across the field and began breaking away with their own attack, Bobby was there, and looking to see if there was any danger from the blind side. It was then, in that match, that he became a great player for me, though, of course, he has always been gifted, yet on maturing became not merely a brilliant individual but also a collective team man."

Ramsey first saw him in full action during the time that he was guiding Ipswich Town from the lower levels of the Third Division up to the First Division, and, quite frankly, he had no love for Charlton or his footballing ability that particular day of Saturday, 25th January, 1958—just twelve days before Munich. I couldn't really blame him, because Bobby torpedoed the Cup hopes Sir Alf had been quietly nursing. A brace of the best sufficed to pitch the East Anglians out of the Fourth Round.

In those days, Charlton was just a youngster, feeling his

way around the professional arena, lacking the big-time experience, yet revelling in the odd first-team spots, and ever so happy and delighted when Walter Winterbottom gave him that first cap chance.

Personally, I have always admired his running, and was especially interested when Ramsey also underlined that facet by saying: "He has always had style and grace, and his running action takes the eye almost every time, particularly as he not only possesses a long stride when in full flight, but can use his feet like a sprinter coming off thc blocks."

I rather gather that the England chief does not rate him very highly when it come to heading a ball, but rightly points out if that line of argument developed that, after all, the game is *foot*ball, and here we have a player of rare balance whether carrying the ball, surviving the tackle, or controlling it, and because of his tremendous speed can slip a ball wide of opponents and then pass them very often quite comfortably.

They say he has never sold a fan short in his life, and so far as I'm concerned that can also be applied to his own club —his one club. Right from his first day of clobbing along the corridors underneath the railway stand he has obeyed the official dictums, and, unlike quite a few I could name, has never caused Matt or the rest of the entourage a moment's unnecessary trouble. Which is a pretty big thing to be able to state of a topline professional of seventeen years. Perhaps he has not gone off the rails because of being planted firmly on them in the formative period when Busby and Jimmy began shaping him, and Bert Whalley, that pleasant fellow of a coach who died in the German snows, used to drill into him the discipline of the field, and forever was repeating himself thus: "If you get into trouble it doesn't do you any good, it doesn't help the team, and it is simply pointless to get sent off, so always make certain you never get on the wrong side of the referee." He's never forgotten that injunction while gradually blossoming like a floret, and if one sees him having a few words with the match official it is always on behalf of some less fortunate team mate whose case he'll be pleading, quietly without any suggestion of correctiveness or danger of being ticked off himself.

Most enthusiasts who have studied his play talk about the effortless control, master of chest-high balls, and the graceful spin away from a tackle, but the red blooded types think of the way he hits the ball when going for the target. It's the block-busters they like. No doubt about it. A Charlton goal pleases everybody at Old Trafford. Except, perhaps the opposing goal-keepers. How do they feel about them? Gordon Banks, generally recognised as England's No. 1, and a man whose great strength is a remarkable positional ability, says: "There's not a lot you can do when he gets one right on the mark, you often know it's coming because you can see him winding up, But the pace of the ball is almost frightening, and you must be near the line of flight to be in with a chance of saving."

One of the nicest things to happen to him was, I believe, the tribute paid by the Brazilian F.A. on the occasion of his hundredth cap. They discovered that Sir Stanley Rous, former F.A. Secretary, and now president of F.I.F.A., was returning home in time for the big game, and persuaded him to act as messenger, carrying an inscribed memento expressing their appreciation of his footballing ability plus magnificent sportsmanship. It was inscribed in twin languages thus: "This is being presented to the most popular footballer ever to have visited our shores."

The ancient State of Jalisco, in the South Americas, heard of that particular event, and, when the World Cup planning awarded England games to Guadalajara, paid special attention to Charlton, and then made him their "Sportsman of the Year." He was the first foreigner to win that honour. The Governor, who himself made the presentation, said it represented a mark of their esteem for Charlton's qualities of sportsmanship and fair play which "set an example his country can be proud of". From these dizzy heights, and after breaking Billy Wright's 105-cap record, he flew home in nice time for attendance at a meeting of the Manchester United Fan Club, which he chairs. And discovered they were also handing him their token—a silver dish to further mark his record number of England games.

We were thinking back to his beginning earlier in this chapter, and I'm now contemplating the day when he first stepped on to the international championship scene, and remember it as a bright Saturday in mid-April of 1958 with England triumphing over the Auld Enemy by four clear goals, quite a performance. He had recovered from the terrible experience of Munich, and was slotting into a line-up of experienced campaigners. Such as Eddie Hopkinson, Jim Langley, Ronnie Clayton, Billy Wright, Ron Slater, Don Howe, Bryan Douglas, Derek Kevan, Johnny Haynes and Tom Finney. Great names of the fifties, when the game was played in the old-fashioned style with players operating largely in their numbered positions without anyone being termed a striker. Or a mid-field man. Or a sweeper-up.

Douglas was his wing partner that memorable afternoon, with the nomadic Kevan leading a line with a left-wing pairing of Haynes and Finney, and he had the tremendous satisfaction of scoring one of the four goals. Yet on the sleeper back from Glasgow, no one was quieter. I couldn't get a peep out of him while all the rest chatted before turning in.

At that time, United's playing list included Wood, Gregg, Carolan, Foulkes, Shields, Greaves, Goodwin, Crowther, McGuinness, English, Dawson, Giles, Pearson, Viollet, Webster and Elms. Apart from Bobby they have all now either hung up their boots or moved on. He is left as the lone Mohican of that decade.

It is now being suggested that he should agree enough is enough, but why should he? We've not got someone here who is breaking up, or too friendly with the scythe of time. The reflexes remain good, the standard high, and he lasts each game as well as the next man. Age alone should never be the final arbiter. Some players are fading in the middle twenties, while others are just as fit and capable going through the thirties. Charlton is one of those.

Anybody with a query about fitness should be introduced to his family life. Then they would often see that even after the most hectic Old Trafford game, Bobby drives home and is quite willing to join in an impromptu affair with local youngsters, or a hectic free-for-all on the lawn with no holds barred. If anybody is puffing or reddening it's not the Charlton boy.

Whenever he does decide to concentrate on something else for a livelihood, and put them into a flat spin at Old Trafford it will be a day of mourning. The whole place will be sorrowing for a man with almost nothing else to win because, after all, in addition to his international honours he also possesses medals from the World Cup, European Cup, F.A. Cup, and League championship, together with English and European " Footballer of the Year " awards. Quite a collection.

That's probably what Ramsey thinks though, if he is on the same wavelength as United he'll not be worrying for a while. One of the last points McGuinness made before stepping down from the team managership was that Bobby could be doing a job for England in the next world series.

Then, after due consideration, he added this comment : " It is quite possible to have the stamina and skill to play for your club, but other qualities are needed in an international team. For instance, the kind of temperament and authority shown so outstandingly over the years by Bobby."

If you require a further opinion, Busby, who has always been one of his greatest admirers, and persevered with him during lean spells when some supporters would have had him replaced, says that though the Billy Wright record of 105 caps which Bobby beat was a wonderful achievement, Charlton's collection is greater because of the fact that he is a forward.

Now that is a theory for the debaters, especially as Matt, one of the top students of the game over nearly three decades, points out that it is always more difficult for a forward to stay consistently brilliant and keep his international spot than it is for a defender.

Having made that point, the club's General Manager, as he is now styled, goes on to say that Charlton continually staggers him with such enthusiasm for so long in one job, and reckons that if the England man stays that way he's never going to grow old, and will always be wanting the ball. And perhaps employing some of the tackling with which he surprised the Rumanians in the last World Cup, when on one occasion, he actually took the ball into three successive block tackles, and came out with it each time. His England team colleague from Maine Road, Francis Lee, noted how the Mexican crowd roared louder with each challenge of this Nobby Stiles stuff, and then later, plainly shaken, immediately called him "Tiger" Charlton. A very unusual sobriquet for Bobby. Very unusual.

Still, maybe not quite such a surprise as when Gordon Banks changed his shirt at the interval after the Rumanians had complained of the Stoke goalkeeper turning out in the usual yellow one. Banks returned to the fray in an England training shirt of brilliant red. When Lee phoned home shortly afterwards, his young son and heir, and the apple of his eye cried out over those thousands of intervening miles: "Daddy, what was Banks doing playing in Manchester United's colours?"

Two final points picture the man and the footballer. We swing the spotlight back to that grim day of tragedy in November 1958. He had been flung from that plane of death, yet, miraculously, escaped with his life, and was immediately worrying about folk back home. So he phoned a newspaper friend of mine on a rationed call, and said: "Could you please let my landlady know I'm all right, and then she'll be able to tell Mum and Dad, in Ashington, and Jack, in Leeds."

Even then, you see, he was thinking of others though whenever I see him and glance at his passport it makes me think that James Bond is just a day tripper to Calais!

Maybe you'll agree he was one of the lucky ones. For instance, Shay Brennan had a harder struggle, though now he's enjoying life on the other side of the channel again as player-manager to Eire League champs Waterford, and felt particularly pleased when signing up his old buddy David Herd, after the well-built Scot had eventually shaken off an injury. He, too, has experienced the strange quirks of Fate, and if you'd like another name for the hard-luck list I'll give you Willie Morgan, the £100,000 three-year-old signing from Burnley, who was dubbed the "Poor Man's Best" over his early weeks at Old Trafford. I think that was because the boy took considerable time settling down and was short of training and troubled by niggling injuries. However, we gradually saw a better Morgan, and there were some occasions when his match performances were ahead of the Best rating.

Ian Ure slots into a more fortunate category because the first-team spot was waiting when he arrived from Arsenal in exchange for a cheque of £80,000, but it was an entirely different life for Brian Kidd, the twenty-one-year-old from the same Collyhurst cobblestone playground as Nobby who had difficulty taming a temper in the early years. The Stretford Enders like him, and that's almost half the battle for any player regularly performang at United's headquarters. They love the way he jousts fearlessly with tough defenders. It reminds them of his famous predecessor, Tommy Taylor, who never stood any nonsense from any full-backs or half-backs.

The trail has been a long one for this youngster who became a United fan in his school days, and was thrilled to join the rest of the starry-eyed boys who were being sorted out in a string of trial games at the mid-week training establishment in Salford. He thought he might become a good player, but there were occasional doubts about the ability to win a team spot, especially when he remembered that already the club had such as Crerand, Law, Charlton and Best in the team.

There were other nagging problems, too, and so one day, while feeling a little unhappy, he actually asked the club to cancel his registration as a schoolboy because of thinking he would never make the grade for them. Fortunately, his suggestion was not acted upon though some time later there was very nearly a parting of the ways because he sought a transfer, and then regretted it. He's always regretted it, especially when looking back and noting with great personal satisfaction how well things have worked out. As they have done. For after catching the eye of Sir Alf he put up great displays at Under-23 level, and, if you remember, was in England's final World Cup pool though later becoming one of the unlucky half dozen to be axed. That's Kiddo, as everybody on the Stretford End will tell you.

NINETEEN

Tough for Wilf

IT WAS really no great surprise to those who knew him well when Wilf McGuinness became Crown Prince of Old Trafford, and then The King, though I'm freely admitting that it did come as a great shock to them all when his reign ended peremptorily after just 140 days of power.

The Board's decision to move him back to the old job of trainer-coach to the reserves, and recall Matt to the team managership until a new man could be named set everyone talking from Land's End to John O'Groat's, and, what's more, split Manchester right down the middle.

It was fairly recognised that successive defeats and a slide to the wrong end of the First Division had set problems which urgently required solving, yet very few folk anticipated that McGuinness would become the twenty-fifth club manager of 1970 to be fired as the Old Year gradually faded out.

Some of the staunchest of United's supporters said he never really had a chance, and it is a fact that the soccer kingdom to which he became heir in the early months of 1969 appeared to be in almost a chronic state of decay and collapse as some of the stars of other and greater years were waning, and many of the new Babes were not quite fulfilling early promise.

The product of the teeming, closely-knit streets of Blackley and Moston, in that tough northern suburban stretch of the city, looked nearly twice his thirty-three years as reporters milled around with smartly angled questions just off the training pitch, and he quietly muttered something about the thin line of difference between success and failure, then quietly added that Manchester United remained his way of life.

That's how it has always been, anyway, since he was knock-knee high to a grasshopper, slightly flat-footed, and admitting he looked a bit like a spider with all arms and legs while playing for Manchester Boys under the critical eyes of Murphy, who didn't exactly fancy that first view, and, to tell the truth, Wilf was not exactly in love with T.Vs first action portrayal of himself.

It is twenty years ago since he came under the influence of headmaster Jimmy Mulligan, at the Mount Carmel Schools, just outside the old village in the hollow, and, like dear Jimmy, was a supporter of the rival Blues, until loyalties gradually changed while getting an extra whiff of the game in an England shirt at schools' and youth levels.

Actually, Wolverhampton Wanderers very nearly collared him. Stan Cullis had heard about young Wilf, and arranged for a visit to the Molineux Grounds, and a look-see at the whole impressive set-up. But, unfortunately for the man who succeeded the great Major Buckley as Master of Molineux, Manchester United came, saw, and conquered at the identical time. It was a match result which changed his life. For it turned Wilf into a follower of the Reds. He became wedded to Busby and all his policies.

He set out once more on the trail which led to England full caps and a league championship medal before taking it on the chin. He broke a leg when only twenty-two. It was the kind of blow which would have finished many, especially when a second operation was necessary, and it became gradually obvious that his playing career was ended almost before it had really begun.

He began anxiously weighing-up the pros and cons of the whole position, particularly worried because of being newly married and facing the usual extra responsibilities. Then the sky brightened. His luck changed. Bill Inglis decided to retire from the post of assistant-trainer, and it was obvious that an intelligent young fellow like himself could prove to be just the type for the job. So he was handed the vacancy, and made such a success of it that the F.A. later appointed him trainer of their youth team, and, eventually, manager of that special pool of starry-eyed youngsters.

All the time, he retained that inborn friendliness and quick smile, and became quite a popular figure at the training headquarters, and downstairs at Old Trafford, where everybody always mixes so well, and the raw youngsters get the same warm treatment as the senior professionals.

For nearly two years, it was rumoured that Busby would be stepping down. He was nearing sixty, and many thought that he might follow the general trend of other walks of life, and let somebody else have a go when that particular stage was reached.

I've no doubt McGuinness wondered about his chances of stepping up, though up to then he'd no real knowledge of club management at top level. Or the responsibility of first-team selection. Or the alertness so necessary for operating in the transfer market.

Yet, when the moment came, the club obviously considered him a good risk. So in the month of April of 1969, McGuinness, one of the earliest Babes, began an apprenticeship for one of the top posts in world soccer. He was a young man called to follow in the footsteps of greatness at a crucial period in the club's history. A time when even finishing second in anything would be considered failure, and it would be nothing short of catastrophic if they fell so low as to be denied European soccer in the immediate future.

There was talent available. There were youngsters knocking at the door. But would the new choice be able to harness the ability and shape it into a new and wonderful combination? He recognised the great problems, and knew he would have to create teams capable of winning, and winning, and going on winning. Or the fans would soon be on his back. Thinking on those lines, he said: "We're not supposed to lose, especially at Old Trafford, because everybody expects us to win, and, of course, that special attitude can create extra problems."

Of course it can—and did. Yet at the start of his brief and exciting reign, Wilf was extremely optimistic. Maybe it would have been thought peculiar if he had not been. However, he finished off that particular season in reasonable style, though must have had some doubts on looking ahead to the next campaign, and recognising that he would be facing quite a number of teams better equipped than United. I was thinking especially of Everton, Arsenal, Leeds, and Chelsea, and also remembering Law's unfortunate and recurring injuries, the goalkeeping worries, and the waywardness of Best.

Close friends often emphasised those factors but he seemed to have them fully measured and tabulated for on reviewing the possibilities of the 1969-70 season he said he felt certain they would win something. That prophecy carried conviction, faith in the future, and was obviously from a clear mind. Unlike a United colleague who was dithering over present selection in a city store at Christmas, and was flabbergasted when the young lady assistant from Pakistan said: "Do you wan' Eddie?" He inquired who Eddie was, and won the sharp reply: "I mean Eddy o' dese?"

When the wrong results began coming along the crowds thinned, once more reminding everybody about the need for success. But he was able to point to the fact that at the end of his first brief sojourn the team had finished eighth in the League, progressed to the semi-finals of three different competitions, and only been knocked out of the F.A. Cup last four by Leeds United, in a second replay at Bolton.

At that point in time, I daresay he looked back, Yes, back to the period when he used to dream dreams. Like all teenagers. But in his case there was generally a man in his sights. The same man. Big Duncan. Whenever he examined the way ahead in those early days, that man Edwards was always there, effectively blocking entry to the left-half position which Wilf was concentrating upon.

Once, the ambitious youngster said there never seemed any hope of forcing a way into the team within ten years, and it was a kind of cloud he was continually under as the formative part of his footballing life saw new horizons, and then experienced only disappointments.

Whenever he watched Edwards in full action there had to be frank admission about little chance of ever being as good a player, let alone better, and, as a transfer request was not to be considered, some other plan had to be examined. That was when he wondered about the remote possibility of Duncan moving to centre-half so that the half-back line could read this way : Colman, Edwards, McGuinness.

That idea always gave him much satisfaction in contemplation, though he readily admitted to himself that both Mark Jones and Jackie Blanchflower might have plenty of criticism. Still, it was one of those thoughts that dreams are made of, and provided him with the maximal of pleasure while making the daily trek backwards and forwards across the town to his homely spot near the Boggart Hole Clough.

He always went on hoping, and eventually got that first big chance when The Big Boy was moved from the No. 6 spot, though it was to inside-forward and not to centre-half, and Wilf stayed put to win his championship medal though, in all truth, still only a reserve and just topping eighteen.

That experience of being a bridesmaid so long made a deep impression. He has always had plenty of sympathy for those on the sidelines, though readily admitting, in the same breath, that it is an occupational hazard in a fiercely competitive business, and becomes more so as most clubs with something good in the bank are building up large first team pools. Which is all right in one way because the majority are being handed first-team wage packets—but not first-team soccer.

That relatively new fashion had been forced upon managers aiming at the game's honours, but it automatically increased frustration, especially among the boys. Reserve soccer becomes a big bind to all of them after a while, and, naturally, is anything but good for their individual game.

Nowhere has that unsettled state of affairs been more apparent than at Old Trafford. Not just in one season, but over more than a dozen. Last winter, for instance, many experienced players were jostling each other in the long queue for places, and not often being picked. I'm thinking now of around the turn of the year when problems were mounting for such as Nobby Stiles, John Fitzpatrick, Francis Burns, Jimmy Rimmer, Steve James, and John Aston and a host of others.

They were finding their chances fading, and I thought that Aston voiced the private opinion of them all when he said it was just a case of going forward or fading into oblivion

" because another winter of reserve football will kill all the talent there is in me."

According to Wilf himself, Aston was always a special kind of player because of being able to easily adapt himself to tactical plans, whereas it would be difficult to shackle either Charlton or Best, because they are instinctive players, and much of their ability might be destroyed if they were asked to conform too much.

By that time, of course, he was the dictator. The man who decided who should play in the team. For at the start of the 1970-71 season the club upgraded him with the full and complete title of Team Manager, and he later talked of other aspects of the job, and how he viewed everything.

He remembered that the first point to strike him on joining the club as a nipper of only fifteen was the remarkable atmosphere of Old Trafford. It was a special atmosphere which, according to him, stemmed from Busby, and spread throughout the entire club, until everybody was a member of one big family.

The character of the top players, as well as their ability seemed to infect and inspire all the youngsters, said the new boss, until junior games took on the importance of mini cup finals because they all knew that important things were also expected of them.

He believed it was that influence which claimed a grip on everybody, and was one of the most important contributing factors in making United so consistently successful in post-war football. And he also waxed enthusiastically about the scouting system, and the way in which it saves clubs money.

That was just before Joe Armstrong had retired, and Johnny Aston had been given charge of scouting, and forty-three-year-old Eric Walker, the man who discovered English international Keith Newton for Blackburn, had become United's new, top talent spotter. Once an amateur referee, and in civilian life a Salford employment officer, he had scouted eleven years for the Ewood folk, and then had a spell working for Oldham Athletic when Jimmy McIlroy was manager, before joining Burnley and combing the Manchester area.

Everything was set fair with a clean bill of health and bags of enthusiasm when the new season opened, but the hurdles gradually became tougher. They hit a losing run. And while their neighbours and rivals a short distance away were looking good for some kind of prize, United's hopes of joining the happy queue began fading.

Then down they went to Arsenal. And Manchester City. And Second Division Middlesbrough. And Third Division Aston Villa. Ten thousand stayed away. Everybody wondered where it was all going to lead to, and what those in top authority were likely to do about it.

McGuinness lost his crown. He stepped down to coach the reserves once more, and Busby took charge while they searched for a new man to take the helm. Some of the players didn't feel too happy about things. One or two said they'd not only let down the club and Busby, but they'd also let Wilf down because they felt that if they had beaten Villa he might still have been in his job. Perhaps so. Who knows?

But I think that McGuinness, on his part, could merely reiterate the haunting words of the old song—*Que sera, sera.*

TWENTY

The Future

THEY WERE replete with hope while lining up for the start of last season, and, indeed, all the available facts pointed to the possibility of a good time. No less a person than Matt himself underlined that when he glanced back at the previous campaign.

Maybe it had been a winter of discontent for some, though not exactly McGuinness, who in his first months in charge of the team had taken them to F.A. and League semi-finals, only losing the senior battle to Leeds, and the other to Manchester City after tremendous struggles.

The Boss admitted they were " desperately unlucky not to win one of five semi-finals, and any talk of it being a disappointing season could hardly be farther from the truth ". That was right. They had nothing to display on the boardroom sideboard, yet the boys had performed heroically while most weeks injuries forced unwelcome changes, or contributed to wrong results. So United moved off again in August of 1970 with Matt operating in the background as the new General Manager and Wilf in complete charge of all team matters.

Everybody in football wondered what kind of a season that of 1970-71 would turn out to be, especially when they found the early going tough. For even in the opening month they were taken apart by Derby in a one-sided Watney Cup final, went down to Leeds in the first of their home League fixtures, then were dealt with in a clash with Arsenal, at Highbury, and luckily salvaged a point at West Ham's expense.

The bright spot came in a midweek night trip to Burnley where, after taking the field as a team with only a solitary point and no goals to their credit, they hit two in a six-minute spell, and, of course, scored a shock win to help boost a morale which had taken a really hard knock.

Unhappily, that livelier form too often deserted them in the succeeding weeks. As they neared the turn of the year relegation clouds were beginning to obscure the view, and, in fact, on 19th December only four other clubs were below them at the wrong end of the First Division—West Ham, Nottingham Forest, Blackpool and Burnley. The danger was becoming obvious to all, though I don't think that anybody even then could imagine United sliding out of a top circle they had graced for so long.

Actually, United and Arsenal are now the only two clubs with the proud distinction of unbroken First Division membership since the pre-war era, and so far as Old Trafford is concerned they have now completed twenty-six consecutive seasons in the top layer. So it was easy to understand the worries of officials and supporters, particularly when the record book revealed that only five of twenty-two games had been won up to the middle of December, by which time this fantastic and unwanted goal average had been built up—24-34. It came from form which split my family of fifty per cent United fans, and the rest City, though my youngest daughter Hilary was only concerned whether she would get to the Cup Final for another close view of the Queen!

Whichever way one looked at the position, however, it was grim, and made more unbearable by the fact that just over the way their arch rivals Manchester City were then among the title chasers though, admittedly, some distance behind Leeds United, and, equally important, were still in Europe.

One day, Jeff Astle, the England and West Bromwich leader, climbed on the platform and said it was the worst Manchester United team he had ever seen, and then the order for crepe mourning went forth because they were knocked out of the League Cup by Third Division Aston Villa.

That was the worst humiliation of years. I well remember how badly the club felt when beaten by lowly-placed Norwich City, Hull City and Bristol Rovers nearly a couple of decades ago, but Villa was only an outfit with a Third Division label. You may probably guess the depression in the coach on the return journey, and how such a sensational result spotlighted the question of team managership all over again. For that reverse marked yet another stage in the general slump.

Attendances were dropping for the first time in over a quarter of a century. This club which had broken all seasonal records of British football with an *average* "gate" of over 57,000 was having to be satisfied with far less. The figures were going down gradually to 45,000, 40,000 and less, and for the first time since the early fifties there were spaces on the terraces and in the stands.

It was probably to be expected because the majority of present day fans, especially the younger ones, have been nurtured on a wonderful diet of success. They have hardly known anything about failure, least of all succumbing to smaller fry, and when it happened they didn't like the taste. So, just as small boys dislike those handing out the medicine, they began staying away on match days, which was something that had never been contemplated in previous years.

Yet thousands took the day off, or slipped away early from office and factory for that trip to the midlands, confident in the hope that their favourites would at last carry the second leg of the Football League Cup semi-final. A defeat by 2-1, and a losing aggregate of 3-2 was something very few had anticipated. It went down very badly. The more so when one reflected that the ultimate decider was schemed by one of United's discards—Willie Anderson. There were only eighteen minutes left, and the overall score was 2-2 when Willie cut loose on the left, centred, and left-winger Pat McMahon nodded the ball home.

Christmas was coming up fast, but there were no festive feelings around that old ground which has witnessed so many wonderful occasions. The players reported for training stints automatically, just as they had always done, but the bottom seemed to have fallen out of everything.

Something had to be done to stop the slide before it gathered momentum, and ended in disaster. There had to be remodelling, either of playing strengths or managerial appointments. Or, perhaps, panic buying of new stars. In the event, Matt told the board he was prepared to shoulder the burden once more though coming up to his sixtieth year.

McGuinness paid the high price of soccer failure after having had a go for just eighteen months—a mere five months as full team boss. And even the hardened newspapermen who gathered around the thirty-three-year-old for an impromptu Press conference in the cold and the biting wind of the training ground just after the change-over had been announced felt sorry for Wilf at that moment of his young life.

They recognised the unseen battle the former England wing-half was waging within himself as he stood before them. Alone. He looked up at leaden skies, glanced quickly at the semi-circle of scribes, and raked a spot of loose soil with a nervous toe cap. Then he said, ever so quietly: "I would bleed for United, though this is disappointing. But managers are judged by results, yet with a bit of luck we might have been in three cup finals."

That was so. He had piloted United to three semi-finals within twelve months which was a feat any other club chief would have regarded as a miracle, but which to United was failure. They have no time for those clubs who trumpet around about progress in this and the other competition yet, in the end, fail to grab a prize of any kind. If no trophy has been annexed by them at the finish of a campaign, then somewhere along the line things have gone wrong, and it's been a winter of failure.

Wilf went back to the job of coaching reserves, which must have been a tough proposition to accept. And Matt, saying his piece in the board-room where so many important gatherings have been held in my time, said: "I might not win a match until the end of this season because you never can tell in this game, but I am sorry it has not worked out for Wilf as he was my choice. But he has still a career in front of him, and, whatever the disappointment, this has been an experience for him, and is something he can benefit from."

It was suggested in different quarters that dressing-room unrest might have pressurised the decision, and it did seem as if Wilf did not see eye-to-eye with all the players, particularly some of the stars. Once, he was engaged in a heated public argument with Denis Law, and it was a fact that within the space of just a few months several players asked for transfers, and others were considerably upset at being dropped.

Whether that had any real effect on the general situation can only be a matter of conjecture, but, apart from Cup progress, cold figures showed that Wilf's teams lost 20 of 65 league games, winning only 19 for a goal total of 99-58. Hardly the kind of record generally associated with the club in post-war years.

Of course, everything might have been far different if United had met with any real success in all their efforts to strengthen the team. I know they made no fewer than eight strong bids for different players, and were turned down in all instances. Even when the offers topped £100,000.

It was obvious, therefore, that when Matt was taking over once again he would have to rely on the men already available while improving the league position. At the same time there would have to be thoughts about another new manager to solidify any gains, and it seemed to me that it would have to be a brave man to step into the breach, though when one cogitates the difference between the brave and the foolish in most sports it is often only marginal.

When Matt resumed control, his first task was to decide the line-up for the F.A. Cup Third Round replay with Middlesbrough. Everybody waited excitedly to see whether he might play for safety with the old hands, or strike out and gamble on switches. As it was, Matt gave a vote of confidence to the team which had been in action in the original tie at Old Trafford, and it didn't repay him with the victory so earnestly desired. Instead, the Ayresome boys slammed the European door in United's face, winning by the odd goal of three.

That was another gloomy trip home, but the game had revealed more scoring potential, and greater emphasis on attacking football, which Matt always believed in and won fine dividends with, especially his favourite 4-2-4 set-up. All those who place high values on wingless wonders are out of tune with this man.

Gradually, the team began to look more like Manchester United, slowly climbed up the league, completely putting all relegation fears behind it, and, of course, those missing fans wandered back as the club joined the top eight, and most of the players recovered better form. In saying that I am particularly thinking about John Aston and Willie Morgan. Both were twice dropped by McGuinness, and, in fact, experienced very tricky passages throughout the first half of the last season.

Morgan had found life rather difficult playing in only nine League games last winter before the change at the top turned the page, and put him in such good humour with himself that supporters who had been critical began changing their opinions, realising for the first time that here was a winger worthy of the fee the club had paid.

It was almost the same for young Aston, and, naturally, with two wingers playing well and fighting hard for the ball the rest of the team began feeling on better terms with the world.

Matt had all the time felt deeply for McGuinness, and also conceded that he had not really wanted to shoulder once more all the worries that go along with that position, and particularly in an age when the pace and the pressures were becoming too great, especially for someone nearing sixty, and still in a state of recovery from Munich. Additionally, he admitted that when the wrong results were piling up the worry was nearly driving him mad, and it was murder staying out of the dressing-room.

That was quite understandable. Because for nearly three decades he had been very closely involved with the United team, and, apart from the period of absence immediately after the plane crash, was always the regular caller both before, during and after a game. It was not entirely a question of talking tactics, but of personal contacts with all the players, interval advice when winning, losing, or remodelling because of injury, and then congratulations or sympathy as the boys dressed for home.

They were match-day missions which developed into not only a regular habit, but a very necessary one. Dressing-room visits are most important, these years. They are a serious part of a schedule for a highly commercialised business. Not like they were between the wars when managers used to stroll in, call out: " Get stuck in, boys, and give 'em a bit of boot ", and then stroll out. That was the style of many I knew.

I've often watched Matt walk stern-faced into the dressing-room half an hour or so before the start of a game. He was even more serious on " Derby " days, or before important cup-ties. As a man who always does every job thoroughly, he was fully involved during dressing-room discussions. So one can appreciate that to suddenly know it is none of your business what goes on in the dressing-room must have been a shaker. It obviously was to him during the time that McGuinness held the reins.

In addition, there was the George Best saga which included unfortunate clashes with authority, and a sudden and unusual penchant for missing vital trains that ended with a club suspension.

That was always on the cards after the Irishman had missed a training stint and the noon train to London for a January game with Chelsea, but it was a surprise, nevertheless. It caught me off balance when a friend excitedly phoned for information, saying that a newspaper contents bill was shrieking out: " George Best Shock ". At first, I thought he said " George Best Shot ". Then I realised what it was all about.

Anyway, those turn-of-the-year worries finally faded when, after being fined £250 by one F.A. Commission, he won the next hearing, making history by being the first player to be proved blameless by a TV film showing. He also apologised to Matt, whom he termed " a real father figure to me ", and added that so far as he was concerned he was playing for the greatest club in the world, and the day I leave Manchester United will be the day when they tell me they don't want me any more.

It was a peace that was welcomed throughout the soccer world. There is no doubting the extraordinary ability of the youngster from Belfast, nor his fantastic pulling power, though here we have a very unusual idol in another way. He is a loner.

Best has many good friends, but he is quite happy on his own. You might say he's the exact opposite of Cassius Clay. No loud talker, he rarely says anything on his own behalf, and off the park has almost always been a law unto himself, living a life which differs from the rest of his Old Trafford colleagues. Yet, at the same time, he is one of the most sincere of people, and suffers the tortures of the damned when out of form and the team is losing.

On that particular point, Alan Ball, Preston manager and father of Everton's World Cup man, said he thought that Best had almost been lost to the game and then brought back by Matt not only to figure prominently once more, but also to play for the team instead of trying to do so much on his own.

This manager who has worked wonders at Deepdale, and possesses considerable knowledge of the problems and headaches facing all club bosses, was full of praise for the United chief. Recalling that most had first been asking what had gone wrong with Manchester United and then what had gone right, Ball said that so far as he was concerned the answer to that conundrum was to be found in just five words—the magic of Matt Busby.

It was his view that the players became different because Matt had the quality which only one in a score of managers possesses : the ability to get players to respond and almost die for the red shirt of United.

Many others expressed similar sentiments as the 1970-71 season drew to its close, and the talk eventually turned for the nth time onto the type of man to take over such a world class club, and fit into the patriarchal set-up where all the key men have either risen from their own ranks or been aces in the pack many years, and are bound together with intense loyalties.

Dozens of likely names came into all those discussions, but

close examination always provided some reason for ultimate deletion of the majority. It was soon very patent that the board was also having difficulty about a short list when, suddenly, in March, the job was advertised throughout the length and breadth of the country. In all its long history, it was the very first time that the club had advertised for a manager.

It was easy to read between the lines. They did not intend repeating their first error of appointment, nor limit its scope. And why not? This was not just an ordinary vacancy. It was not the managership of some hard-up, struggling organisation that wanted a new man, but one of the wealthiest, best supported, most respected and successful clubs in world soccer.

That's no exaggeration. This is a club which has been a major prizewinner or runner-up in no fewer than fourteen of the twenty-five post-war seasons, a record far out of reach of any likely challenger.

It's been made by top stars of the Home countries, who with just the odd exceptions have all been products of the Busby Grooming Academy and, incidentally, have taken their outlook and values from a boss who must have had an understanding with the mythical Phoenix, because twice he has built a new club from the ashes of the old.

Always remember that Old Trafford lay in bomb-blitzed ruins in February, 1946, when Matt signed his first managerial contract while still in khaki, and raised it to the soccer peaks. He did it a second time when the team was almost wiped out in the Munich disaster which wrote Finis to so many of his high hopes of that era.

Now, a new page of that tremendous history is about to be written because the nadir is past. And, that being so, it seems to me the right time for referring to a copy of the club's programme of 28th August, 1937, which lies before me at this moment.

A contributor of those pre-war days wrote this remarkable piece: "Manchester United stands for something more than any person, player, or supporter because it is the soul of an organisation which goes on making history season after season. . . ."

What kind of history will it make this winter? It's future is in the melting pot once more—but, I think, a great future by any measurement or assessment.

No one could guess what lay ahead, but everybody interested in United's future felt reasonably happy at the start of this season, anyway. That mood came about largely because of having signed off the last campaign with such a resounding victory over their old rivals and neighbours.

Knowing the way in which these "Derby" clashes are viewed not only at board-room and dressing-room level but also by the milling thousands of soccer enthusiasts in this sport mad centre of the North-west, there is no doubt in my mind that such a favourable result greatly helped all Old Trafford fans to reach happier terms with themselves for another winter.

This one moved off in the absence of one of the old campaigners. A Busby babe of many years ago. McGuinness. Wilf wondered if Greece might prove kinder and give him a better break, so he resigned from the staff and flew overseas for a fresh beginning.

Well, the Greeks have a word for it. I can't exactly remember it at the moment, but when I was last over in Macedonia they, like us, believed in that old maxim about fortune favouring the brave.

If that turns out true in this connection, Wilf should be on hand for a generous ration of good luck, because, after all, he had the guts to suddenly turn away from all the friends of years, and have a go at a job where the language difficulties will always provide an additional problem to the many facing a foreigner, even among friendly people.

He'll find them just as keen on the game as we are on this side of Europe, but should not present himself in social circles as an admirer of the works of George Bernard Shaw, because they have never forgiven the famous old man once saying that Greek scholars were privileged men because few knew Greek, and most knew nothing else.

Anyway, Dr. Hadji Georgiou, the affable president of the Aris Salonika club, who have signed McGuinness, is very optimistic about the chances of success inside the span of a two-year contract, and says that the former United man will have a completely free hand, pick the teams, and so on.

I would say, therefore, that everything is in his favour. I'll add that if he wins the right hallmark I know that nobody—yes, nobody—will be happier about such success than Matt, who has seen so many of his boys move into managerships, though not always enjoying the modicum of luck which is so very necessary in the peculiar job of running a professional football club.

This is the kind of post which somehow always appeals to all the fans. They just consider the glamour, and the wonderful trips abroad, and the banquets. None is aware of the real problems of agreeing with four different views at the same time; sitting on the fence and placating directors, players, supporters and the newspaper boys.

It's because of ignorance of the day-to-day routine and heartbreaks that almost every time a manager's job falls vacant the mail immediately swells with applications from men in practically every walk of life—bus guards, bacon curers, postmen, window cleaners, engine drivers, city clerks, landscape gardeners, plumbers, butchers, bakers, and so on.

Anyway, let's hope Wilf has luck. That's what United also need this time round. Loads of it. For there must be triumph in this season of 1971-72. That's not just my humble opinion, but represents the general view of all the club's supporters.

They are hungry for something to crow about once more after successive campaigns have left them with nothing to show, whereas over the previous twenty odd years hardly a winter passed without the team gaining a trophy of some kind or another.

All that wonderful period had an unexpected effect. It educated them to anticipate something almost as an automatic reward for attendance, and there you have yet another headache a boss must always anticipate at Old Trafford.

Loosely interpreted, it means that a manager can pull his guts out and take the team to a runners-up spot in the League, or the last-two stage in a Cup competition yet be branded a failure if there is no winner's prize at the end of it all.

Anyway, now we are off again after a summer which has been regularly punctuated with newspaper "think" pieces about the need for appointing a new team manager, likely candidates for the very hot seat, and divided opinions on the trickiness of working on the same staff as Matt.

Anybody's guess seemed as good as the rest when the vacancy came up for discussion, though constant mention of some names must have caused tremendous embarrassment to their owners, even after denials of any interest in the job.

It is known in the game, of course, that occasionally newspapermen fly kites for friends who may be interested in the Sits Vac column. They sometimes do so even when the man concerned does not have a cat in Hell's chance of landing a particular job, because the publicity often wins him a wage rise with his present employers.

Juggling of names was perhaps to be expected, and it developed into an intriguing pastime because out of all the managers earning a living out of football, these days, not much more than a handful are outstanding. And they are mostly built-in with their present outfits, and couldn't get away if they wanted to move.

Matt heard about the stories suggesting there might be difficulties for a new boss, and that was only to be expected because he has always been a man who moved around in a wide circle. But the position was soon clarified because he is joining the board.

He admitted not wanting to end a close relationship with the dressing-room, but decided to do so on commonsense grounds as he grew older, and the game is a young man's game.

So the way ahead for Manchester United became crystal clear. There was a signpost to success. A winter of endeavour to be negotiated. Matches to be won. The old jealous pride to be restored with a weather eye cocked on Europe all the time.

Everything is there for the achieving. What a wonderful prospect for Frank O'Farrell. What a challenge. What possibilities. He may need a light touch of the Blarney Stone now and again, but it will be only a consummate knowledge of men and the game which will finally work the oracle.

After the friendly Irishman had been appointed to the vacancy by the Manchester United board, there were some who were sorry that the club's new team boss was not Sir Alf Ramsey. Or Dave Sexton. Or Jock Stein. I was not among them because it's my opinion that O'Farrell could become just as great as any of those.

His references were good, anyway. First there were many years spent as a classy wing-half battling at various times for Preston North End, West Ham United, and his beloved Eire. Then as manager he had a tough apprenticeship with Southern Leaguers Weymouth, a fine stint with hard-up Torquay, and a brilliant period with Leicester City.

It was December 1968, when this dark-haired son of County Cork, who barely reaches up to 5 feet 8 inches in stockinged feet, turned his back on countless friends around Tor Bay and headed north for the Midlands.

Matt Gillies had left for Nottingham Forest, the Leicester club was hungry for honours after a shuttlecock existence in the fifties, and the many problems of Filbert Street were tossed into his lap.

He got away to a mixed start. They slipped back into the Second Division, and lost the F.A. Cup final to my old friends of Manchester City. But within twelve months the team finished just a couple of points short of promotion, and, as you know, moved up again as champs last May.

That was a performance which automatically spotlighted a big clue to the man. He resisted the temptation to imitate many other bosses and talk of greater triumphs on the way. Instead, there was just the smile of satisfaction with a job well done, and warm appreciation of the boys' efforts.

That's the way it will always be. Boasting is out. Excuses, too. Results and figures will tell the tale now. Even great triumphs will not provide a ladder for mounting rooftops and shouting the odds. It will be that way all the time—honest talking, endeavour, and expertise. A great combination which, for a man of forty-two, is unlikely to undergo any real change.

I rate his background first class, particularly the handling of players and their moans, and there's always been shrewd assessment of the transfer market. His views and personality constantly impressed Busby, who once said: "He always seems to know what he's doing, and I especially like the way he handles difficult situations."

Matt could have added that the new manager recognises there are times when everybody fancies taking the easy way out, but underlines there is no room for such attitudes when the target is the top.

I would bet he is probably deceiving most of those who are meeting him for the first time this winter, because his pleasant mannerisms and easy Irish style always supply an impression of softness sans discipline. But they are merely an inheritance from the friendly folk in and around Cork, Kerry, Tiperary and Limerick.

It may be thought he'd never even frown at a referee's decision because his brogue is as soft as a leprechaun's smile, yet Frank O'Farrell can match up to a tiger when correction is an urgent and vital necessity.

Chapter One of the *new* Manchester United is now being written . . .